Thames Path

Phoebe Clapham is a writer and
editor. She lives in East London.

Thames Path
in London

Phoebe Clapham

with photographs by Katherine Clarke

Aurum

in association with

NATURAL ENGLAND

For Andrew, most delightful of walking companions

Published in 2012 by Aurum Press Ltd
7 Greenland Street, London NW1 0ND
in association with Natural England.
www.naturalengland.org.uk
www.nationaltrail.co.uk

Text copyright © Phoebe Clapham 2012

The Thames Path Extension from the Thames Barrier to Crayford Ness, and the two circular walks in this book, are not part of the official Thames Path National Trail administered by Natural England.

A catalogue record for this book is available from the British Library.

ISBN 978 1 84513 706 9

Book design by Robert Updegraff
Printed and bound in China

Cover photograph: *Battersea Power Station* © Jason Hawkes/Corbis
Half-title page: A Slice of Reality, *created by Richard Wilson in 2000, Greenwich Peninsula*
© Paul Carstairs/Alamy
Title page: *City of London skyline from Butlers Wharf* © Justin Kase zsixz/Alamy

Aurum Press want to ensure that these National Trail Guides are always as up to date as possible – but stiles collapse, pubs close and bus services change all the time. If, on walking this path, you discover any important changes of which future walkers need to be aware, do let us know. Either email us on **trailguides@aurumpress.co.uk** with your comments, or if you take the trouble to drop us a line to:

Trail Guides, Aurum Press, 7 Greenland Street, London NW1 0ND,

we'll send you a free guide of your choice as thanks.

Contents

Circular walks: pages 41–3 (in Richmond Park) and 124–6 (from Limehouse)

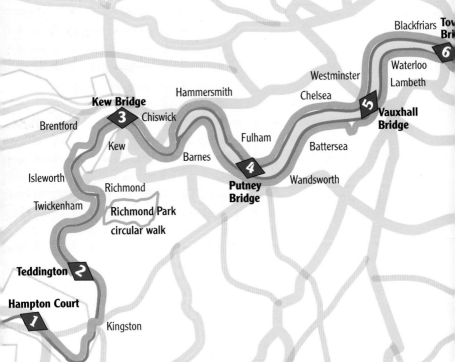

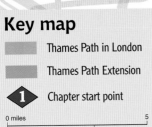

Key map

Thames Path in London

Thames Path Extension

1 Chapter start point

0 miles   5
0 km   5

Blackfriars Tow
                   Bri
                        6

Waterloo

Westminster   Lambeth

Hammersmith   Chelsea

Kew Bridge
3   Chiswick

Brentford   Fulham   5   **Vauxhall
                                                            Bridge**
Kew   Barnes   Battersea

Isleworth   4

Richmond   **Putney**   Wandsworth
                Bridge
Twickenham   **Richmond Park**
             circular walk

Teddington 2

Hampton Court
1   Kingston

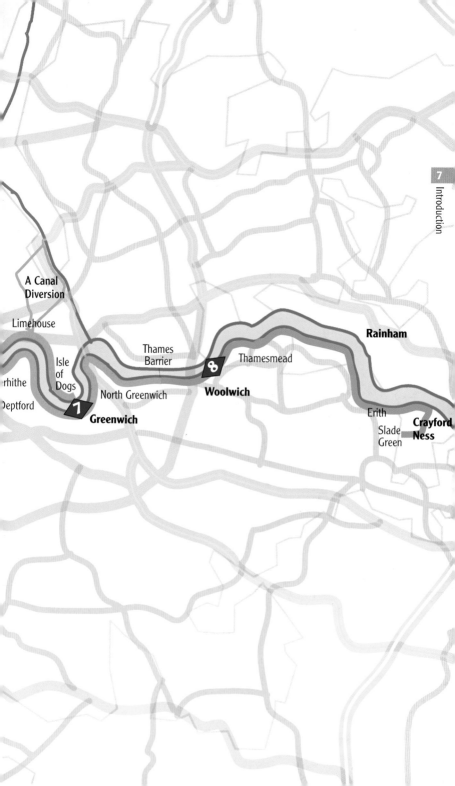

**A Canal
Diversion**

Limehouse

rhithe

Isle
of
Dogs

eptford

Thames
Barrier

North Greenwich

1

Greenwich

Thamesmead

Woolwich

Rainham

Erith

Slade
Green

**Crayford
Ness**

Introduction

The London section of the Thames Path is unique amongst National Trails. Instead of rugged mountains and ancient forests, you will encounter an urban landscape formed by two thousand years of human history, some of the world's most famous buildings, and sweeping vistas along a river whose character varies dramatically, from the rural tranquillity of Richmond and Kew through the bustle of Westminster and the City to the swiftly changing Docklands and the industrial reaches beyond.

This guide takes you right through London, from Hampton Court in the west to Crayford Ness in the east, a total distance of 50 miles (80 km). Between Teddington (where the tidal river begins) and Greenwich the path runs on both sides of the river, with many bridges enabling you to cross between the two. The Thames Path proper ends at the Thames Barrier, near Woolwich, and the remaining 10 miles (16 km) are part of the separate Thames Path Extension, marked on signposts as a sailing barge rather than the familiar acorn.

Unlike most other long-distance walks, the Thames Path through London can be easily accessed at almost any point. The eight chapters in this book each begin and end near a station (as do the two circular

walks written especially for this guide, which start in Richmond and Limehouse respectively), and there are many other public transport options available between. The path is mostly paved and entirely on the flat, and hence attractive to walkers of all ages and degrees of fitness. Pubs, cafés and restaurants are numerous, and there are many opportunities to break off from the path and inspect an enticing church or museum.

The constant variety of the Thames Path offers something for everyone. The Thames plays a vital ecological role as a wildlife corridor, home to many different species of bird, from the familiar herons and cormorants to exotic Egyptian geese and peregrine falcons that sometimes roost on Tate Modern. Just as important are water-loving plants and insects, and the fish that have returned in droves to the Thames since its waters have once more acquired the capacity to sustain life after many decades of pollution.

The London Thames is also strikingly scenic. The graceful curves and wooded banks of the river as it runs through Twickenham and Isleworth attracted the poets and artists of the 18th century, and are still lovely today, with tree-fringed aits (islands) in the middle of the river, and the occasional skyscraper in the distance to add contrast. Erith Marshes, on the Thames Path Extension, is one of the few saltmarshes to survive in south-east England and has a strange, uncanny beauty in the evening light.

However, perhaps the most obvious attraction of the Thames Path is the unparalleled opportunity it offers to explore the history of London, England, Britain and the wider world.

A signpost in Richmond, where the Thames Path meets the Capital Ring.

Old Father Thames: a mid-18th-century statue by John Bacon the younger, in front of Ham House.

History of the London Thames

London exists because of the Thames – the tidal river, easily accessible from the English Channel but also highly defensible, first drew the Romans to settle on the shores of what is now the City, later enabling London to become the hub of global trade. From the Emperor Hadrian (a bronze head of whom was found in the Thames in 1834) to the Blitz and the redevelopment of the Docklands, the Thames has been integral to London's story, and as you make your way along the Thames Path you will pass innumerable sites and buildings that have played a central role in English and British history.

The Thames bears one of the oldest place names in Britain. It was known to the Celts as *Tamesis*, meaning 'smooth running water', and at some point acquired its own god or protector, Old Father Thames, who is depicted by several statues along the river. There

are traces of human habitation along the London Thames dating back as early as 4000 BC – wooden piers by the south side of Vauxhall Bridge, still visible at very low tides – and it first enters the history books in 54 BC, when Julius Caesar invaded, crossing the river with his army to defeat the British tribes lined up on the other side.

London itself was established a century or so later, with the first timber bridge across the Thames built in around AD 52. It soon became a significant port, though the departure of the Romans in the early 5th century dealt a serious blow to its fortunes. However, the site remained strategically attractive, and in the 7th century the Saxons built a new settlement a little further west, by what is now Aldwych.

In about 886 King Alfred the Great re-established London and built Queenhithe dock, and in the early 11th century King Cnut started to build a palace where the Houses of Parliament now stand, soon to be joined by Westminster Abbey nearby.

One of the sturgeon lampstandards that have lined the Albert and Victoria Embankments since 1870.

Pool of London below London Bridge, and the river banks on either side crowded with wharves and warehouses to store the innumerable goods in transit between London and the rest of the world. Downriver were the shipbuilding centres of Limehouse and Blackwall and, from the early 16th century, the great royal dockyards of Deptford and Woolwich. As central London became busier and more polluted, the rich moved westwards, to fine new mansions by the river in Chelsea, Fulham and Chiswick, and in the 18th century many owned a villa in Richmond or Kew as a weekend and summer retreat.

By the early 19th century London was becoming not just a capital city but a world metropolis. Central to this process were the vast docks, built in Wapping, Rotherhithe and the Isle of Dogs at the cost of thousands of people's homes.

For many centuries the two settlements remained separate, with Westminster as the heart of government and London the commercial centre. Across the river was Southwark, from early times the entertainment quarter, with theatres, bull-baiting, brothels and taverns galore.

Until 1750, when Westminster Bridge was opened, the only fixed crossing between the north and south sides of the river was London Bridge, the gates of which were locked at curfew time. Moreover, roads were narrow, muddy and crowded, meaning that the most efficient way to travel anything but short distances was generally by boat. Public buildings and private houses were constructed right on the banks of the Thames, with river steps (many of which can still be seen) leading down to the water's edge, where boats would be moored.

As London grew, therefore, it sprawled along the Thames in both directions, with its commercial life centred on the

Meanwhile, the role of the Thames in London's life was changing. Better roads, the invention of the railways, and a flurry of new bridges across the Thames meant that the river was no longer the most efficient means of transport. Massive increases in population and the swift growth of industry placed an increasing strain on the capital's infrastructure, and in the 1860s and 1870s the great engineer Joseph Bazalgette changed the face of the Thames for ever with the construction of the Victoria, Albert and Chelsea Embankments, which gave London a functional sewerage system, new wide roads running along both edges of the river, and underneath them, on the north side, the new underground railway.

The Thames' role was not yet over. Although in central London buildings started to turn their backs on the river, repelled by unpleasant odours and industrial waste, below Tower Bridge the docks were busier than ever, handling more than a third of the nation's trade by 1937. The Second World War came as a bitter blow to the capital, as elsewhere – London's seaborne commerce fell to a quarter of pre-war levels, and German bombers set the docks on fire night after night, destroying half their storage capacity and of course the lives of hundreds.

After the war recovery seemed swift, but it was not to last. Although, under the influence of campaigning and new legislation, pollution levels began to fall – in 1974, to great excitement, a live salmon was found near Teddington – the role of 'London River' in the nation's trade was almost over. The growth of container shipping meant that the London docks were just too

All hell let loose: the docks ablaze following the first raid of the Blitz in September 1940.

small and inconvenient for the new age of ocean transport. In 1981 the last dock closed and the capital's remaining maritime trade moved to the port of Tilbury, downstream towards the Thames Estuary.

In the early 1980s, the London Thames seemed almost irrelevant to the capital. Barring the occasional tourist boat between Westminster and Greenwich, the river was almost abandoned – though marine and bird life was gradually creeping back. The old docks themselves lay deserted, mile upon mile of abandoned tracts of empty water and forgotten industrial machinery.

Then everything began to change. The London Docklands Development Corporation engineered a massive redevelopment programme and, within a decade, Canary Wharf had ceased to be an obscure trading quay and had begun to symbolise a new hub of global finance. New blocks of flats sprang up along the river on both sides – some more aesthetically successful than others, but all bringing fresh life to the Thames and its shores.

Meanwhile, the South Bank, home to the Royal Festival Hall and National Theatre but traditionally rather

uninviting, was revitalised with cafés and restaurants, its popularity helped by the London Eye, erected in 1999 and now a much-loved part of the capital's skyline. Nearby, Shakespeare's Globe, painstakingly designed to imitate the theatre the playwright had performed in four hundred years earlier, and the transformation of the derelict Bankside Power Station into Tate Modern, meant that the south bank of the Thames was suddenly the place to be.

At the same time, the river has regained – if modestly – its role as a transport artery: several thousand commuters travel to work each day on the flourishing Thames Clipper boat services, and barges can frequently be seen carrying building materials and waste between central London and the industrial sites downstream. A sustained focus on the natural environment means that the Thames is now one of the cleanest metropolitan rivers in the world, and there are many innovative projects along its banks – such as the 'green jetty' by the O2 Arena, and the new nature reserve planned for Purfleet in the east. There are always potential risks on the horizon, but for the moment the Thames' future seems bright.

A Thames Clipper zooms through central London, bearing commuters to work in the City.

Claude Monet's Study of Waterloo Bridge at Dusk, *1903, with smoking factory chimneys in the background.*

The Thames and the arts

Probably the most famous works inspired by the Thames are the much-loved children's classics *Alice in Wonderland* and *The Wind in the Willows*, which have their birthplaces further up the river, in Oxford and Pangbourne respectively. However, the London Thames has inspired many works of its own, most of them grittier in nature. Perhaps the most famous is Charles Dickens' *Our Mutual Friend*, which opens with the unforgettable scene of a body being dragged out of the river near Southwark Bridge; throughout the novel the narrative is drawn back to the Thames at moments of drama. Dickens' *Great Expectations* starts just as memorably on the bitter Kent marshes, and later sees the hero, Pip, row all the way from Temple Stairs past the docks into the estuary, in the hope of smuggling the convict Magwitch abroad (a scene marvellously realised in David Lean's 1946 film). For Sherlock Holmes addicts, Arthur Conan Doyle's *The Sign of Four* features the great detective and Dr Watson in a spectacular chase along the Thames in a steam launch.

The river's artistic heyday came in the 19th and early 20th century, when painters including Alfred Sisley, James McNeil Whistler, Claude Monet and of course the sublime J. M. W. Turner devoted months on end to capturing the changing light and character of the river, from Molesey and Hampton Court on the south-west edge of London to the docklands and the Thames estuary itself. Several of their paintings are reproduced in this book, representing only a minute proportion of the riches out there, many examples of which can be seen in London's museums and galleries (notably Tate Britain, which houses a vast collection of Turner's works).

The fascinating enclosed world of the docks has kindled many imaginations, not least those of film-makers. *City of Ships* (1939) and *Waters of Time* (1951), both available on DVD, document the Port of London in its heyday, with a sublime confidence that London will always remain the capital of global trade. Even more enjoyable is *The Pool of London* (1951), a thriller that starts with a merchant ship docking just west of Tower Bridge and proceeds to feature a criminal heist in the City, a car chase through the Rotherhithe Tunnel and copious footage of the lonely streets and towering warehouses of the old docks. Very unusually for the period, its most likeable character is a black Caribbean seaman.

The docks are gone; but the Thames continues to inspire writers, artists and musicians, as it has since Edmund Spenser immortalised it in 1596 with perhaps the most famous line of Thames poetry ever written: 'Sweet Thames, run softly, till I end my song.'

A longer list of books that feature the Thames is included in the Further Reading section, page 153.

Shakespeare's Globe, on Bankside: a rigorously detailed reconstruction of one of London's first theatres.

The Thames Path

In his booklet *A Guide to the River Thames*, published in 1983, Adrian Prockter begins, 'For those who do not work on the river, the buildings which line the Thames are some of the least known in London . . . probably because few people have easy access to the shoreline.' Things are very different today, and for this we have to thank the River Thames Society and the Ramblers' Association, whose campaigning and planning finally brought about the adoption of the Thames Path as a National Trail in 1987.

Since then enormous efforts have gone into ensuring that as much as possible of the London Thames is accessible to walkers. Walk London has done sterling work promoting the Path and ensuring that signage is clear, and, since London regained its own governing body in 2000, the Mayor and Greater London Authority have explicitly supported public access to the riverside. Even more importantly, individual boroughs have required all new developments beside the Thames to include a riverside promenade accessible to the public.

The battle is not quite won. Funding cuts threaten future investment in the route, and developers often shut sections of the Path for months if not years at a time, requiring frustrating detours. Let us hope that enlightened attitudes prevail and that future generations in their turn have the chance to enjoy London's river.

Planning and safety

One of the many joys of the Thames Path is its accessibility. It is pretty hard to get seriously lost and, apart from parts of the Thames Path Extension, one is rarely more than half a mile (and usually much less) from a station or bus stop, meaning that if a member of your party gets tired or the weather turns nasty you can beat a swift retreat.

However, London is, as it has always been, in a constant state of redevelopment. At various points the Thames Path is diverted to avoid building sites; in the lifetime of this

A signpost for the Thames Path Extension near Tripcock Ness; note the sailing barge logo.

book some of these diversions will no longer be necessary, and others will arise in their place. Keep an eye out, and be prepared to follow diversion signs, or work out your own diversion using the map where necessary.

For most of its length the path is easily traversed by walkers of all ages and degrees of fitness, and much of the path is paved and therefore accessible to wheelchair users, small children in buggies and wearers of unsuitable footwear. I have indicated in the text where there are steps, and have tried to point out a step-free route where possible. If you are planning to cover a long section then it is of course advisable to wear sensible shoes and take a jacket and umbrella to guard against the ever-unpredictable British weather.

There are no serious hazards on the path (unless you count the occasional kamikaze cyclist), but it is worth noting that the path between Teddington and Kew floods at high tide – do check the tide times on www.tidetimes.org.uk before setting out, especially if your party includes people who might find it hard to scramble to safety. Similarly, although crime of any sort is very unusual, you may want to avoid walking along some sections of the path alone after dark; the eastern stretches of the path in particular can feel rather isolated.

Eating and drinking

There are countless pubs, cafés and restaurants on the Thames Path, and often your problem will be too much choice rather than too little. However, there are also several stretches of a couple of miles or more where there are no options at all, so do plan ahead. For most of the path, with the exception of the Thames Path Extension east of Woolwich, you should have no problem finding newsagents or corner shops where you can buy water and emergency rations, though you may have to leave the path itself and strike inland for a minute or two.

Inevitably some eating places are better than others, so I have tried to note particularly historic, scenic or just plain good pubs and cafés along the route. All recommendations are based on personal experience, but remember that standards can rise or fall very quickly.

Cycling

Much, but not all, of the Thames Path is also open to cyclists, mostly by means of a dual-use path (sometimes divided into a pedestrian lane and a cycle lane), but occasionally via two parallel paths. Individual boroughs decide whether cyclists are allowed on the Thames Path or not, so watch out for signs. Even when cycling is allowed, pedestrians take priority on off-road sections of the path, and cyclists should always be careful and considerate, and ring their bells to ensure pedestrians are aware of their presence.

Where the Thames Path is not open to cyclists, there is usually an alternative route nearby – look out for blue National Cycle Network signs. Detailed cycle guides of London and the Thames are available from Sustrans at www.sustransshop.org.uk.

Transport

Londoners love to complain about their public transport, but in fact London's is a pretty impressive network, and certainly much better than anywhere else in Britain. Services are usually fairly frequent and reliable, but both underground and main lines are often closed at weekends for engineering work, so make sure you check on www.tfl.gov.uk (for underground and DLR) and/or the relevant train company website (most likely to be South West Trains, on www.southwesttrains.co.uk) before you set out.

All underground, Docklands Light Railway and train stations are marked on the maps in this book, and there is a large-scale map of the whole route on pages 6–7. Bus stops and routes are not marked (there are just too many) but you should be able to find a bus stop, usually with map, on most main roads. The TfL website has information on all bus routes, and if you have a smartphone there are several useful London bus apps with real-time details of services.

The most convenient way to pay is by Oyster card, which offers both season ticket and pay-as-you-go options. You can buy Oyster cards at tube, DLR and some train stations, and they're valid on London Underground, DLR, all train stations within London, buses, trams and Thames Clippers. To top up your Oyster card, go to a station or look out for newsagents displaying the Oyster Ticket Stop sign.

There are also many boat services up and down the river; the journey is enjoyable in itself, and there is a particular pleasure in walking along a stretch of river and then taking the boat back again. Thames Clippers are the leading passenger boat company, running services from Vauxhall through Central London to Woolwich; check www.thamesclippers.com for times. There are also various small companies that offer specific services, such as Hampton Court to Richmond, or Westminster to Greenwich – see Useful Information, page 152, for full details.

Visitor attractions

There are many, many museums, art galleries, historic buildings and the like along the London Thames and open to passers-by, from Syon Park and Westminster Abbey to Kew Bridge Steam Museum and Firepower! In fact, if you walk the whole length of the London Thames you will pass several of the greatest visitor attractions in Britain, if not Europe. There are also numerous less well-known museums and churches that turn out to be a delightful discovery (the William Morris collection at Kelmscott House in Hammersmith, the Garden Museum in Lambeth and the Rose Theatre spring to mind, amongst many others). Such places add an extra layer of enjoyment and interest to your trip.

I have tried to give an idea of their characteristics and schedules, but do check opening houses in particular in advance. Several of the top museums and galleries (including Tate Britain and Tate Modern) are free, which means that it is entirely feasible to nip in for an hour, admire some masterpieces, have a cup of tea and then get back on the path. Museums run by local authorities are also free (Fulham Palace and the Greenwich Heritage Centre are particularly recommended). Other attractions are expensive and exhausting enough that you will probably want to dedicate a few hours to them, but it is perfectly possible (not to mention enjoyable) to spend a morning walking and an afternoon going around a historic house or gallery, or vice versa.

The two museums most closely associated with the Thames and its history, both of them revelling in spectacular collections and both of them free (except for special exhibitions) are the National Maritime Museum in Greenwich and the Museum of London Docklands, which is situated off the Thames Path at West India Quay. The National Maritime Museum is home, alongside lashings of naval history and the Royal Observatory, to a fascinating Maritime London gallery. The Museum of London Docklands, housed in a characterful warehouse in West India Quay, might just as well be described as the museum of the Port of London. Its galleries are handsomely and imaginatively designed and, in addition to all the historic photographs, maps and displays one would expect, it features an impressive reconstruction of old dockland streets and shops.

Best section of the Thames Path for . . .

Historic interest: Chapter 5 (Vauxhall Bridge to Tower Bridge) both sides.

Working river: Chapter 8 (Woolwich to Crayford Ness).

Industrial history: Chapter 6 (Tower Bridge to Greenwich) south side.

Period charm: Chapter 3 (Kew Bridge to Putney Bridge) north side.

Rural beauty: Chapter 3 (Kew Bridge to Putney Bridge) south side.

Accessibility: Chapter 2 (Teddington to Kew Bridge) south side.

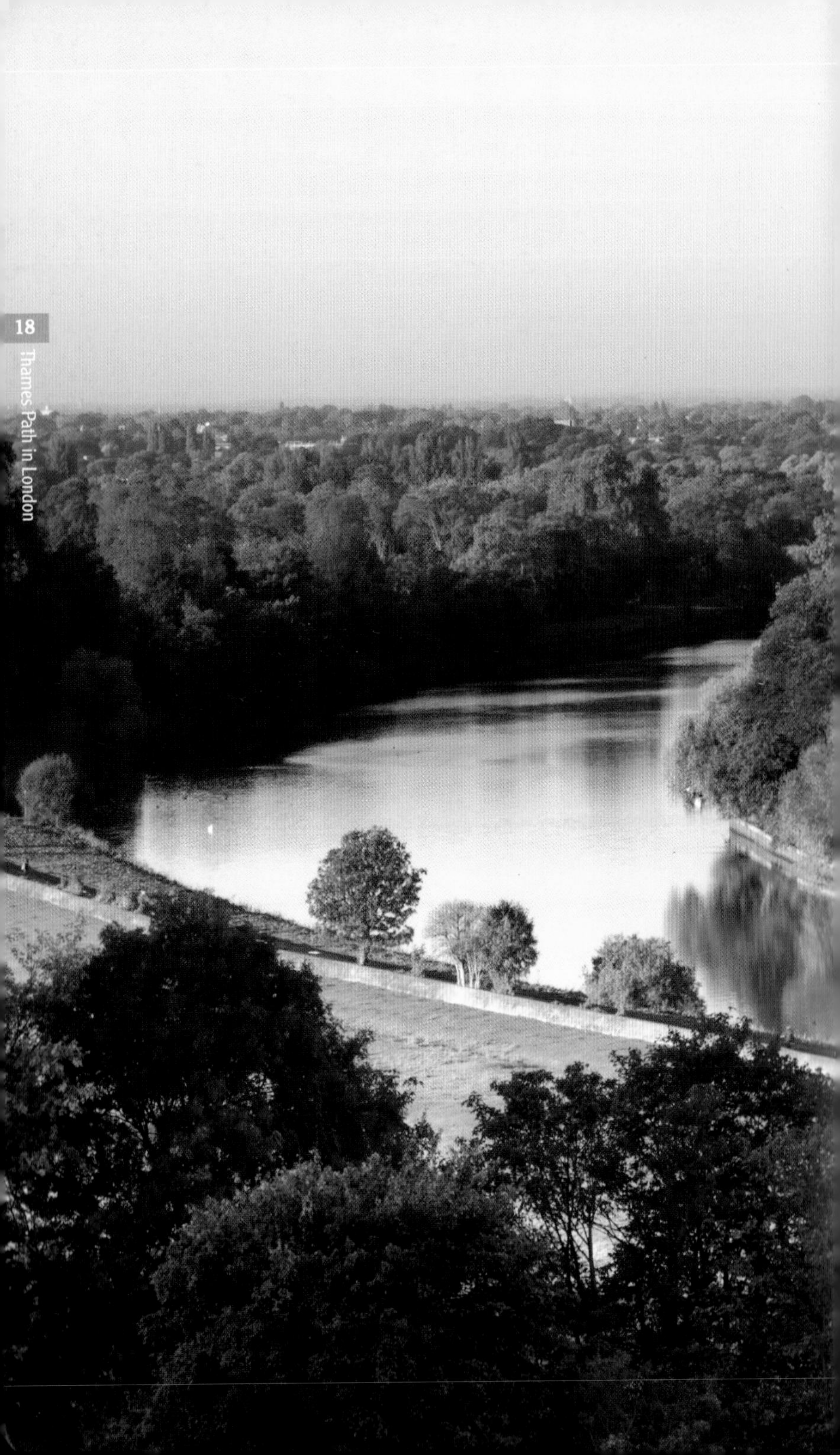

Thames Path
in London

Hampton Court to Teddington

5 miles/8 km
(Hampton Court to Kingston 3 miles/4.8km,
Kingston to Teddington 2 miles/3.2 km)

Turn right out of Hampton Court station and cross the handsome 1930s bridge, designed by Edwin Lutyens and W. P. Robinson of reinforced concrete and, unusually, faced with red brick and topped with stone balustrades to mirror Hampton Court itself. At the other side, turn right along the lane running parallel to the river, known as Barge Walk after the barges that used to moor up here. You are now officially on the Thames Path. On your right is the Turk Launches pier, from which regular boat services leave for Kingston and Richmond; on your left is Hampton Court, one of the great palaces of Tudor England.

A little further on you'll see Hampton Court Pier, offering cruises all the way to Westminster with Westminster Passenger Service Association. On the left just beyond it is the handsome crenellated Banqueting House, built in 1700 for William III's private entertaining and in later years used by royal children as a playhouse. When the brick wall on your left gives way to modern railings, look back through the gilded gates for a magnificent view of the 17th-century façade of the palace and its meticulously planted formal gardens. For many years this would have been the first sight most people had of Hampton Court, as they came down the river from London.

Across the water you'll see a channel flowing into the Thames, past the corner of what is known as Cigarette Island – this contains the combined Mole and Ember rivers.

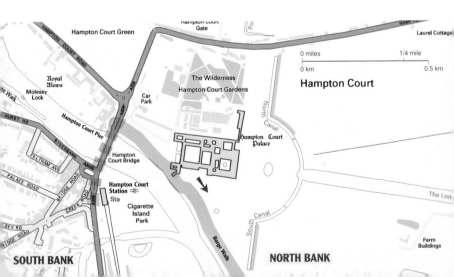

Hampton Court

Hampton Court was originally built for Cardinal Wolsey, one of Henry VIII's chief advisors, in about 1514, drawing on Italian Renaissance architectural principles alongside more traditional late Perpendicular Gothic, but in 1528, as Wolsey's star began to wane, he gave the palace to the king. Henry enlarged it with a great hall, enormous kitchens and a real tennis court (all still in situ today), and spent large parts of the remainder of his reign here. One of the gatehouses is named after Anne Boleyn (whose apartments were still being built when Henry had her summarily executed), and it was at Hampton Court that Henry's son Edward was born, at the cost of Queen Jane Seymour's life. The ghost of his fifth wife, Catherine Howard, is said to walk in the Haunted Gallery, from which she was dragged screaming when Henry heard of her adultery, to be beheaded like Anne Boleyn before her.

Hampton Court continued to play a significant role in royal life. Charles I was imprisoned here by the Parliamentarians in 1647, only to escape down the Thames and away to the Isle of Wight. By the late 17th century the palace was beginning to seem old-fashioned compared to the glories of Versailles, and William III and his wife Mary II commissioned Sir Christopher Wren to rebuild it. Wren designed the grand Baroque Fountain Court, encompassing the beautifully decorated state rooms that still exist, before Mary died of smallpox and William lost interest in the project. George I and George II ordered further redecorations, carried out by Vanbrugh and William Kent accordingly, but George III hated the palace (apparently because his father, Frederick, Prince of Wales, had once hit him here) and no monarch lived here again. Instead, it was divided up into grace and favour apartments for retired loyal servants of the crown; some still remain, their little doors visible in unexpected corners of the palace complex.

Hampton Court Palace is now, of course, a major visitor attraction; the famously tricksy Maze is a perennial draw, but just as enticing are the palace's magnificent interiors and its beautifully tended grounds, stretching over more than 750 acres.

Hampton Court Palace from the river: one of the great glories of Tudor England.

Ahead the path divides into a wide, surfaced lane on the left, much used by cyclists, and a narrower track alongside the river – take whichever you prefer. Already the road noise is dying away, to be replaced with honking geese and chirping songbirds. The path continues through beautifully tended parkland, with ashes, alders and tall black poplars spreading overhead. On the other side of the river is Thames Ditton Island, which can be reached only by pedestrian bridge or boat.

Continue following the path, past a row of low wooden stakes. The river here is as narrow as you'll ever see it within the area covered by this book, with the opposite bank so close you can hear the music and chatting of people in their gardens across the water. Note the little

wooded ait (islet) on your right – you'll see many more of these along the western stretches of the London Thames. The word 'ait' is a contraction of 'eyot', a Middle English term meaning 'little island'. The path follows the river's curve to the left, passing a peculiar brick cylindrical structure, and the view starts to become more urban, with cars and commercial buildings visible on the other bank, in contrast to the sylvan prettiness of the Thames Path itself.

Look out for a large Victorian building with a crenellated tower beside it on the opposite bank; this is the splendidly named Seething Wells, originally home to the Chelsea and Lambeth Waterworks Companies, which built filter beds here in the 1850s to purify river water before piping it to London

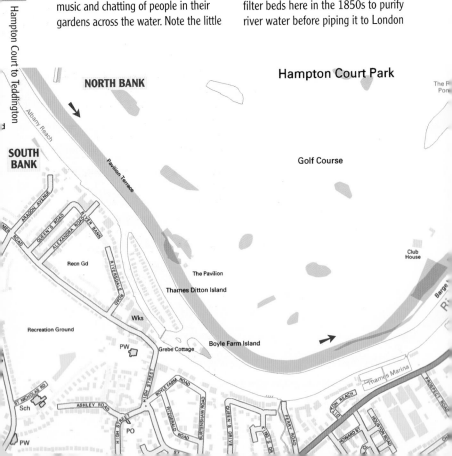

The Thames near Hampton Court, wending lazily downriver.

for use. The site has recently been sold off by Thames Water to a private developer. A little further on, also on the other side, is Harts Boatyard, which runs a ferry across the river at weekends.

Just beyond it you'll see Raven's Ait. Now home to an 'exclusive island venue catering for weddings and corporate functions', it has an unusual history. For many years it housed a Navy League boat training school, before being redeveloped as a conference and wedding centre. This closed in 2008, whereupon the ait was occupied by squatters who sought to turn it into an 'eco-centre' for London. Alas, they were evicted in May 2009 and the island reverted to business use, though at least the Sea Scouts remain.

Beyond it on the opposite bank is a church tower in an exuberantly Italianate Renaissance style – this is St Raphael's Roman Catholic Church, built in 1847–8, less than 20 years after the Catholic Emancipation Act gave English Catholics their civil rights back.

Continue following the lane until you reach Kingston Bridge. There has been a bridge across the Thames at Kingston since at least the 12th century, and until Putney Bridge was built in 1729 it formed the only fixed river crossing between London Bridge and Staines Bridge, 14 miles (22.5 km) upriver. Today's bridge, completed in 1828, is a dignified structure of Portland stone. Cross over it and take the steps down on the right-hand side, passing underneath the bridge and then out on to the riverside plaza. To your right, behind a glass wall in the basement of

John Lewis, you can see some rare surviving remnants of old Kingston: a barrel-vaulted cellar from a 14th-century merchant's house (note the lovely chequerboard flint and chalk walls) and, on its left, the stone walls and pier of the 12th-century bridge.

Follow the promenade along the river and around Turks Pier, from which regular boats leave for Richmond and Hampton Court, then left along a lane and under the battered railway bridge. Continue straight on into Canbury Gardens; the path alongside the river is a designated (and much-used) cycle track, so you're probably better off on the broader avenue just above it. In the middle of the park you will skirt round the ever-popular Boaters' Inn (which has public toilets inside). When you reach the edge of the park, follow the quiet lane that runs along the water's edge.

Kingston Bridge, built in 1828; the brick underside is a nice touch.

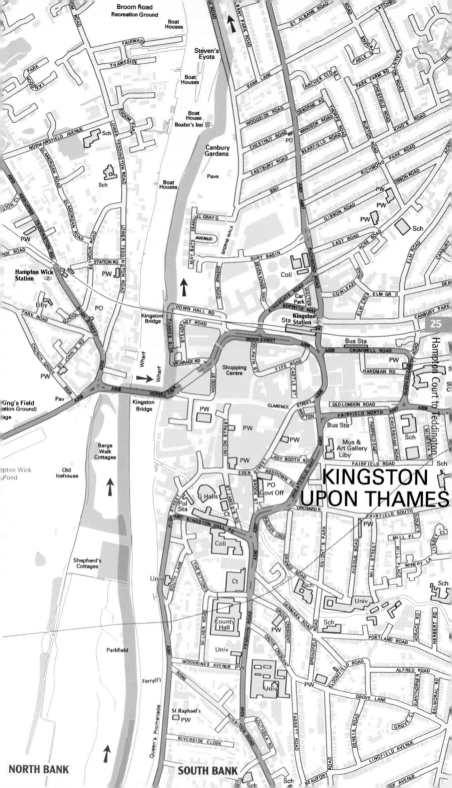

KINGSTON
UPON THAMES

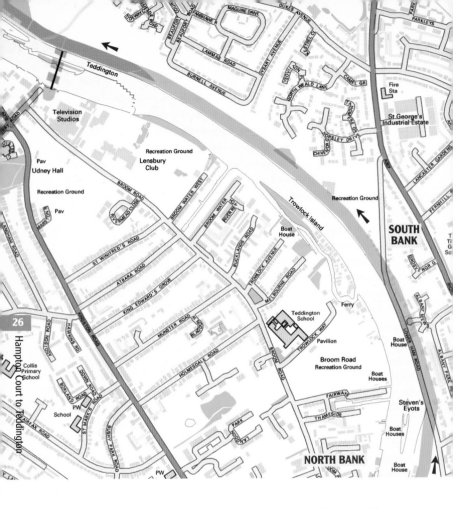

After a few hundred yards the lane veers off to the right; follow the left-hand path into the park ahead of you. The spreading horse-chestnut tree just beyond the entrance is known as the Half-Mile Tree, from the distance to the centre of Kingston; it was planted in 1952 to replace an ancient elm tree with the same nickname. The gravelled path runs along the water's edge, shaded by the alders, sycamores and willow trees above. You may need to repress a spasm of envy for the people living in the houses on the other side of the river, with their picnic tables overlooking the Thames and boats moored at the end of their gardens.

After the best part of a mile of pleasant walking, you will see ahead the slightly intimidating spectacle of Teddington Weir, with an enormous lock complex just beyond it. This is the point at which the tidal river begins and this section of the walk ends.

To get to Teddington station (see map on page 29), cross the footbridge to the north side of the river and keep straight on up Ferry Lane and the High Street, turning left down Station Road just before the roundabout.

Boating Mania

You may think that pleasure boating on the Thames is popular today – there is certainly no lack of small yachts and sailing boats, narrowboats and canoes. But in fact its heyday was more than a century ago, and the most popular spot of all was just here, far enough away from central London to feel charmingly rural, but easily accessible by train from Waterloo. On a sunny summer's day in the late 19th century many thousands of enthusiastic city-dwellers would travel down and hire a rowing boat or punt for a few hours of innocent diversion – their pleasure possibly increased by the fact that this was an easy way for young men and women to mingle in groups without censure or supervision.

Such was the popularity of this pastime that it inspired the classic account of Thames boating: Jerome K. Jerome's *Three Men in a Boat*, first published in 1889 and never out of print since. It tells the story of how the narrator, J, along with his friends George and Harris and their unimpressed dog Montmorency, set out on a boating trip from Kingston upriver to Oxford. Jerome originally intended to write a serious travel guide, but almost immediately the manuscript developed a life of its own, and

the result is – even today, more than 120 years later – one of the best comic novels in the English language.

Here is Jerome describing the scene in Molesey Lock, which can be seen just upriver from Hampton Court Bridge:

> On a fine Sunday it presents this appearance nearly all day long, while, up the stream, and down the stream, lie, waiting their turn, outside the gates, long lines of still more boats; and boats are drawing near and passing away, so that the sunny river, from the Palace up to Hampton Church, is dotted and decked with yellow, and blue, and orange, and white, and red, and pink. All the inhabitants of Hampton and Moulsey dress themselves up in boating costume, and come and mouch round the lock with their dogs, and flirt, and smoke, and watch the boats; and, altogether, what with the caps and jackets of the men, the pretty coloured dresses of the women, the excited dogs, the moving boats, the white sails, the pleasant landscape, and the sparkling water, it is one of the gayest sights I know of near this dull old London town.

Molesey Regatta, 1894: boats, more boats and still more boats!

2 Teddington to Kew Bridge

NORTH BANK: Teddington to Kew Bridge 7½ miles/12 km
(Teddington to Richmond 3½ miles/5.6 km, Richmond to
Kew Bridge 4 miles/6.4 km)

SOUTH BANK: Teddington to Kew Bridge 5¾ miles/9.25 km
(Teddington to Richmond 2¾ miles/4.4 km, Richmond to
Kew Bridge 3 miles/4.8 km)

> **WARNING: The south
> bank of this section of
> the Path is prone to
> flooding at high tide.
> Check the tide tables
> before you set out at
> www.tidetimes.org.uk
> and take the alternative
> route described here if
> necessary.**

North Bank

*From Teddington station, take the exit via
Platform 2 and turn left down Station
Road. At its end, turn right down the High
Street. After the shops and cafés peter
out, the road becomes Ferry Road. Note
the diminutive brick St Mary with St
Alban church on your left, and on your
right an enormous church in the French
Gothic style of the 1880s, formerly St
Alban's but now deconsecrated and
converted into the Landmark Arts Centre.
Ahead you will see the gold chains of the
pretty Teddington Lock Footbridge; turn
left down Manor Road before you reach it.*

Manor Road becomes Twickenham Road
and then Strawberry Vale, a clue to the
nearby presence of Strawberry Hill

House, one of London's oddest but most
fascinating buildings. It was designed in
the mid-18th century by the writer,
politician and aesthete Horace Walpole,
a devotee of Gothic style whose
imagination conjured up a riot of
turrets, battlements, fan vaulting and
stained-glass windows. After many years
housing St Mary's University College,
Strawberry Hill has now been restored
and reopened to the public, who can
visit on Saturday to Wednesday
afternoons, April to October.

Continue along the road for several
hundred yards, until you reach a mini-
roundabout. To see Strawberry Hill, turn
left up Waldegrave Road; otherwise,

The Barge Lock at
Teddington, the largest lock
on the non-tidal Thames.

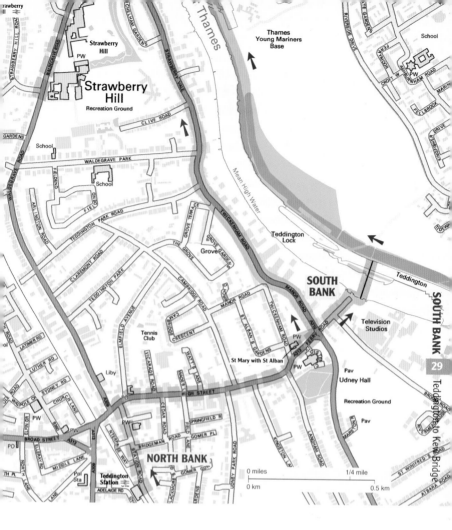

South Bank

From Teddington station, follow the directions on the opposite page, then continue to the riverside and cross the two-part footbridge over the Thames.

Turn left towards the locks that separate the tidal from the non-tidal river. This is the largest lock complex on the Thames, with three separate locks, one of which, the Barge Lock, is long enough to host a veritable flotilla. Past the lock, the path continues along the river, with pretty woodland on your

right. A few hundred yards on you'll see a fenced-off stone pillar bearing a sign saying 'Thames Conservancy Lower Limit 1909' – this marks the boundary between the Environment Agency's jurisdiction over the river and that of the Port of London Authority.

A little further on, cross a bridge over a lock, with a boating lake on your right. On the other side of the bridge you enter Ham Lands nature reserve, a lovely stretch of trees, undergrowth and open grassland on the site of turn right just after the mini-roundabout into Radnor Gardens, which are home to a summerhouse and a gazebo from Walpole's time. Turn left through the park to admire them, then right towards the river, past a statue of a soldier commemorating local men who died in the First World War. Turn left along the river, only for the path to curve away again and out of the park.

Turn right along the main road and past Radnor House school. Note the bus stop immediately afterwards bearing the name 'Pope's Grotto', after an enterprise even more eccentric than Strawberry Hill. In 1720 the poet Alexander Pope designed an underground chamber here, beneath his Thameside villa, and decorated it with geological specimens from all over the country. The villa has long since been demolished but the grotto remains, underneath the school buildings, and can be visited during Twickenham Festival Week in June each year.

Keep on the main road until you come to a junction – this is Twickenham town centre. Turn right and then right again down Wharf Lane and finally back to the river.

As you turn left along the Thames, on your right is Eel Pie Island, best remembered as a 1960s music venue – legendary names including the Rolling Stones, Pink Floyd and The Who performed here in the old Eel Pie Island Hotel. Follow the charming riverside promenade past the Barmy Arms pub (rugby fans particularly welcome), rowing clubhouses and lots of different boats. On your left you will see a church which is an extraordinary amalgam of traditional Kentish ragstone tower and grandiose red-brick nave with pedimented south façade. The church dates originally from the late 14th century, but a combination of neglect and the unwise digging-out of vaults meant that the body of the building collapsed in 1713, and was replaced by a design of the architect John James, whose most famous work is St George, Hanover Square, in the West End. Pope is buried here.

Follow the lane parallel to the river, past Champions Wharf and under a lovely footbridge with a stone balustrade, which joins the gardens on either side of the road. Ahead is the White Swan pub, a free house dating back to the 17th century, though the interior has been recently modernized. The terrace juts out right into the river and at very high tides the water can rise over the road, separating the terrace from the pub itself.

The road continues between idiosyncratic semi-detached villas and lots of overhanging greenery, then past the handsome 18th-century Orleans House, so called because Louis Philippe, duc d'Orléans (and later king of the French) lived there between 1815 and 1817. Now the Richmond-upon-Thames art gallery (free entrance every afternoon except Monday), its most striking feature is the Octagon, designed by James Gibbs in 1720 and boasting an extravagant Baroque interior. It is surrounded by pretty landscaped gardens and the stable block at the back houses a decent café.

From the road outside Orleans House, turn right into a small park and back to some filled-in gravel pits. Keep alongside the river through an avenue of mixed woodland, until, after the best part of a mile, the path suddenly emerges from the woods into a car park, with a magnificent view of the Star and Garter Home on Richmond Hill ahead.

The path (liable to flood at high tide, so take care) continues through parkland – in fact, this is the Ham House wildflower meadow, carefully managed to encourage plants such as lady's bedstraw, yellow rattle and tufted vetch, and the accompanying grasshoppers and dramatically striped cinnabar moths.

The Star and Garter Home on Richmond Hill, occupying an imposing position above the river.

SOUTH BANK

the riverside. Just after you leave the park is the jetty for the Ham ferry, which for a negligible sum bears pedestrians to the other side of the river every weekend and weekdays between February and October. The path continues along the river – note the magnificent run of elder trees, particularly striking in late spring when they are in bloom. Ahead of you on the opposite bank, raised prominently above the Thames and framed by greenery, is the Star and Garter Home for disabled servicemen and women, established in 1916 for men seriously wounded in the First World War. On your left is the exquisite Marble Hill House, built as a country retreat for Henrietta Howard, mistress of George II. Now owned by English Heritage, it is open to visitors on Saturday and Sunday (guided tours only).

At the end of the parkland, a longish wooded stretch follows, with the tarmac path shaded by trees arching overhead and a fine view of the grand villas of Richmond Hill to your right. The vista then opens up a little, with handsome red-brick blocks of flats on your left and more boathouses on the other side of the river. Passing Cambridge Gardens Park on the left, you will see ahead the elegant arched Richmond Bridge, notable for its 'humpbacked' appearance, designed to allow boats to pass under the central span. Opened in 1777, it is the oldest surviving bridge over the London Thames, and for many people the most beautiful.

Arcadian Thames

Until the 18th century, the stretch of the Thames between Hampton Court and Kew was one of rural tranquillity, with little villages running down to the riverside interspersed with farmland and market gardens. As London expanded, however, this peaceful landscape became increasingly popular – both with aristocrats, merchants and politicians, who built country retreats here, and with writers and artists inspired by its picturesque charms. The poet James Thomson lauded 'the matchless vale of Thames', likening it to Arcadia, the pastoral paradise imagined by the ancient Greeks, while Horace Walpole commissioned the fanciful 'Gothic Castle' known as Strawberry Hill, and Alexander Pope created a new, romantic style of garden for his villa in Twickenham, artfully sprinkled with classical statues, secluded groves and evocative ruins.

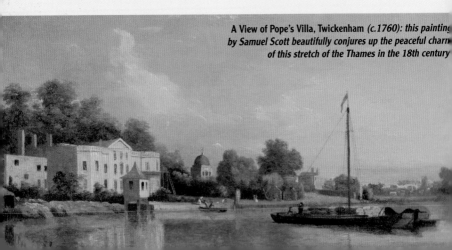

A View of Pope's Villa, Twickenham (c.1760): this painting by Samuel Scott beautifully conjures up the peaceful charm of this stretch of the Thames in the 18th century

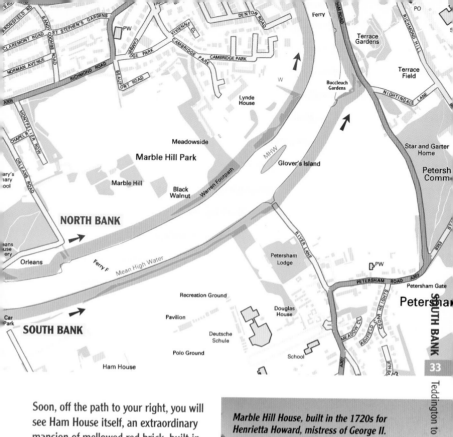

Soon, off the path to your right, you will see Ham House itself, an extraordinary mansion of mellowed red brick, built in 1610 and little altered since 1698. Unlike many historic houses, its interior and furnishings survive almost intact, and it offers a fascinating glimpse into aristocratic life three centuries ago. Now in the care of the National Trust and open every day except Friday from February to October, it also boasts lovely (and carefully tended) formal gardens.

Back on the path, you will pass the ferry to Twickenham, and then see Marble Hill House on the opposite bank. Ahead is Richmond Hill, topped with grand villas. A little further on the river bends sharply left and the path follows it, turning slightly inland. (For the circular walk around Richmond Park (pages 41–3) follow the signpost to Richmond Hill and Park at the entrance to Buccleuch Gardens.)

Marble Hill House, built in the 1720s for Henrietta Howard, mistress of George II.

Just before the bridge, turn inland along the slipway and cross over at the traffic lights, continuing down Willoughby Road opposite. On your left note Willoughby House, a 19th-century villa built from creamy yellow bricks unusual for London, with a whimsical tower modelled on an Italian campanile. Go straight on through scuffed green barriers into Duck's Walk, passing through leafy suburbia, though with no sign of the river. If you're feeling deprived you can turn down the overgrown private walkway opposite Riverdale Gardens, which doesn't lead anywhere but offers a quick glimpse of the Thames.

At the end of Duck's Walk the path passes under Richmond railway bridge, a 1908 steel affair with handsome land arches on either side sporting scrolled keystones, the remnants of the original bridge of 1848. Immediately afterwards is Twickenham Bridge (1933), with thin red-brick bands enlivening its discoloured concrete. A hundred yards further on is the much prettier Richmond Footbridge, cast in delicate yellow and green and actually an afterthought to the lock and weir on the other side. Beyond it begins a paved then tarmac pedestrian path alongside the river, which continues for a few hundred yards. Just after a chimneyed red-brick building, the path turns inland; follow the Capital Ring signpost down the lane then right on to Richmond Road and over a small Thames tributary. A sign welcomes you to Isleworth.

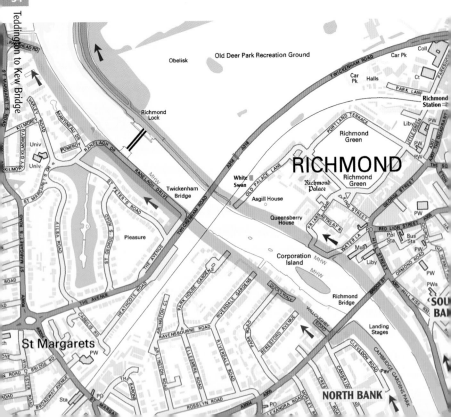

Turn left into Buccleuch Gardens and continue along the riverside promenade up to Richmond Bridge. There are several cafés and restaurants on your right (the Tide Tables Café under the bridge usually has good cakes), and on your left a pier from which Thames River Boats depart to Kew, Hampton Court and Westminster.

On a warm sunny day, and even to some extent on a grey drizzly one, Richmond riverfront is devoted to pleasure – boat trips (scheduled or row your own), bicycle hire, buskers, pubs, ice-cream vans, all overlooked by the handsome 18th-century buildings of Richmond's society heyday. Dragging yourself away (or beating a swift retreat, depending on your tastes), follow the promenade towards the railway bridge. Just beforehand on the right, note Asgill House, built in 1767 as a weekend retreat for the then Lord Mayor of London, and now guarded by walls, spiked fences and some very beautiful white roses. If you fancy a brief detour, turn right here down Old Palace Lane, towards the White Swan pub, and you'll find yourself on Richmond Green, surrounded by gorgeous 17th- and 18th-century buildings and the gatehouse of Richmond Palace, all that remains of one of the greatest Tudor royal palaces, where Elizabeth I died in 1603.

Back on the path, you pass under the railway bridge and then Twickenham Bridge. On your right now is the Old Deer Park, so called to distinguish it from Richmond Park further up the hill, where the deer now live; the Old Deer Park is now home to the Royal

Mid-Surrey Golf Club and the London Welsh RFC.

Continuing along the path, you will soon find Richmond Lock and Weir, built in 1894 in response to the increasingly shallow water between Richmond and Teddington, as a result of which the river became a trickling stream at low tide, causing enormous problems for river traffic and the local fish population. The weir consists of three sluice gates which are lowered two hours after high tide and raised again two hours before the next high tide, meaning that the level of the upper Thames is never less than half its high-tide depth. When the sluice gates are raised boats can float unhindered underneath the bridge; when lowered they must use the lock alongside to pass between the differing river heights.

SOUTH BANK

35

Teddington to Kew Bridge

Follow the unexciting main road around the curve and finally turn right down Lion Wharf Road, with a welcome sighting of boats ahead. Back on the river, turn left towards the Town Wharf pub, with tree-covered Isleworth Ait across the water on your right. The path runs actually along the pub terrace then up to old Isleworth village, with a quick diversion inland to cross the Duke of Northumberland's River. From the bridge the path continues straight on down pretty Church Street, much of it unchanged from 200 years ago.

At the London Apprentice pub the path returns to the river, passing Butterfield House (reminiscent of a diminutive Strawberry Hill) and All Saints Isleworth, which has a 14th-century tower like St Mary's Twickenham, and an almost equally ill-matching nave of red brick and glass. Follow the road inland and turn right through the gates of Syon Park, the property of the Percy family, now Dukes of Northumberland, since 1594. The name derives from

Sion (Jerusalem) and harks back to the estate's previous life as one of the great abbeys of medieval England, until suppressed by Henry VIII in 1539. Syon House is the only great house in the London area still in private hands, but open to the public on Wednesdays, Thursdays and Sundays between March and October (the gardens are open daily during the same period). It's best known for its lovely Robert Adam interiors, and gardens landscaped by Capability Brown, including a lake which is home to breeding terrapins.

To your left lies the parkland, with a small belvedere visible in the distance; to your right the old brick wall guarding Syon House. This stretch is very pretty; in summer it becomes rather crowded at the visitors' entrance to the house and garden centre, but calmer again on the lane that leads away on the other side, signposted to Brentford, with a view of the impressive Great Conservatory, finished in 1830.

Houseboats opposite Isleworth Ait: a typical Thames scene, with mixed woodland on both sides of the river and tower blocks rising in the distance.

Car Park
Garden
Centre

Syon Park

John Busch
School

Lodges

Syon House

Isleworth
Ferry Gate

Cemetery

PWs

Syon Reach

West Middlesex
Univ Hospl

Queen's Cottage
Grounds

Que
Charlo
Cott

All Saints PW   Pav

King's Steps
Gate

London Apprentice PH   Town Wharf

Obelisk

Golf Course

Old Deer Park

King's Observatory

Isleworth Ait

Mean High Water

Golf Club

Nazareth
House
(Convent)

PW
(priv)

**NORTH
BANK**

SOUTH BANK

The path continues onwards, feeling pleasantly rural, with a wooded stream running parallel on its right. For a brief period, when Isleworth Ait blocks your view of the built-up opposite bank, you could imagine yourself in the actual countryside, were it not for the jets thundering overhead. Just after All Saints Isleworth on the opposite bank you'll see a striking pink pavilion – this is the boathouse belonging to Syon House, built by the great architect James Wyatt in 1770. J. M. W. Turner rented a house nearby in 1805 and filled numerous sketchbooks with his watercolours of Thames scenes.

After half a mile or so, just after you see Syon House itself across the river, the vista opens up and for the first time you can see the soaring tower blocks of London proper. Further on, while this side of the river remains idyllic, the other side starts to develop the blocks of flats and general city sprawl that will become familiar if you venture further down the river.

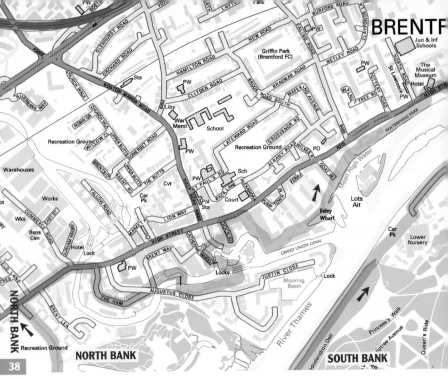

Passing out through the gate, turn right along the unprepossessing main road. Soon you will cross over the Grand Union Canal – admire the locks to your left, but stay on the main road a little longer, turning right down The Ham through a light industrial area. Just after you cross under a road bridge, ascend the paved steps and you'll find yourself alongside not the river but the canal, probably London's second most important waterway. Take the path up to and over another bridge over the canal and then immediately left down the steps (if avoiding steps, keep straight on past the Galba Court flats) and right along the canal towpath and past the Thames lock. Go up the steps at the end of the lock and turn left, then keep straight on over another bridge past the boatyard and along the cobbled lane.

Turn right along the main road, swiftly leaving it again by turning right alongside the Heidelberg building and back to the Grand Union Canal. Soon the path bends left and you follow the canal to its very junction with the Thames. Turn left all the way around Ferry Wharf, then keep straight on through the row of bollards, with the San Marco restaurant on your left. The path returns momentarily to the river before turning left up to Brentford High Street. Turn right to follow the High Street briefly but unpleasantly, then right again down a broad flight of paved steps (keep to the road if you're avoiding steps) and left through a pair of blue half-barriers, then right to the riverside at last. Ahead are some narrow stairs, which take you to a raised waterside promenade and then gently downhill again.

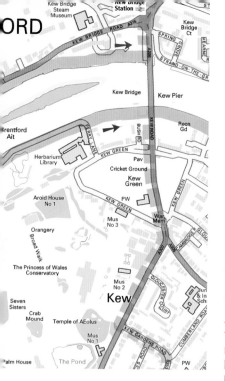

ORD

gardens are also extremely popular with visitors, who can admire Kew Palace (built in 1663 by a Dutch merchant and later bought by King George III) and Queen Charlotte's Cottage alongside the many conservatories and the treetop walkway that enables visitors to ascend right into the tree canopies. The riverside entrance to the gardens is in the car park a little further on, opposite the junction with the Grand Union Canal on the other side; however, you may want to make a separate visit in order to make the most of the many attractions (and the not inconsiderable entrance fee).

Ahead on the opposite bank is the tower of the former Kew Waterworks, now the Kew Bridge Steam Museum; keep on the path and you'll soon reach Kew Bridge.

If you are ending your walk here, take the steps up to Kew Bridge. For Kew Bridge railway station, cross the bridge, then cross over the traffic lights and turn left. For Kew Gardens underground station, turn away from the river along Kew Road, passing Kew Green; turn left down Kew Gardens Road and then left again down Station Approach.

On your right now, though totally sequestered by the trees in between, is Kew Gardens, or the Royal Botanic Gardens to use their proper name. In existence for more than 250 years, the gardens cover 121 hectares and house the world's largest collection of living plants. A major scientific centre, the

The junction of two great waterways: the Grand Union Canal meets the Thames in Brentford.

The path continues through Watermans Park, with a lawn on your left and, on the road above it, a sweet little church with a battered 15th-century tower. This is St Lawrence, the oldest church in Brentford, which is now deconsecrated and seems – unforgivably – to have been left to rot. You return to the road at the Musical Museum (an extraordinary collection of 'self-playing instruments', including a Mighty Wurlitzer organ, and open Tuesdays to Sundays and most Bank Holiday Mondays). Just a few yards on, look out for the overgrown flight of steps heading downwards to your right; these will lead you back to the riverside.

Continue along the narrow path. On your left you'll see a fine Italianate brick tower topped with a neat cupola – this was built as the standpipe tower for the pumping station established here in 1838, which from 1855 drew its water from upriver in Hampton and filtered it here before piping it into west London. The pumping station is now the excellent Kew Bridge Steam Museum, which houses a fine collection of stationary steam engines, many still in working order, and open from Tuesday to Sunday. Keep on the path until you reach Kew Bridge.

For Kew Bridge station, turn left up to the main road and cross at the traffic lights to the far side; the station is on your left.

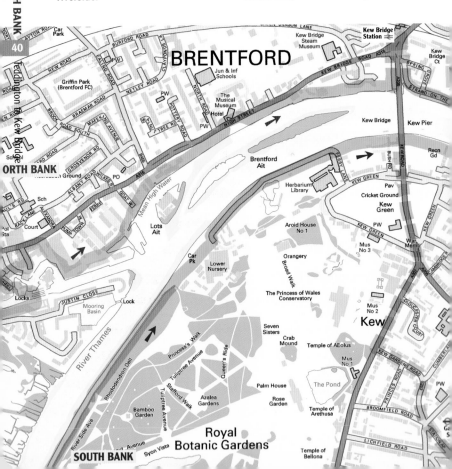

Richmond Park: a circular walk with deer and parakeets

The suggested walk is 3 miles (4.8 km), but this can easily be shortened or lengthened according to preference.

From Richmond station, turn left up Kew Road, which soon becomes The Quadrant. At the traffic lights go straight on along George Street. At the road junction, turn left up Hill Street, which leads to Richmond Hill, with its spectacular views over the Thames and beyond. Just after you pass the Royal Star and Garter Home on your right, continue through the gates into Richmond Park.

From the Thames Path, turn off at the end of Ham Lands, at the entrance to Buccleuch Gardens. Instead of turning left along the riverside promenade, follow the signpost to Richmond Hill and Park, straight up to the main road. Turn left to cross the main road at the traffic lights, then right back along the road and left up Nightingale Lane. Follow the lane as it winds left past the Petersham Hotel, then turn right at the top up Richmond Hill and enter Richmond Park via the gates ahead.

Richmond Park, the largest of all London's royal parks at 2,500 acres, was originally part of the vast Manor of Sheen, where Edward I held court and Henry VII built Richmond Palace on the banks of the Thames. Charles I moved his court to Richmond in 1625 to escape a bad outbreak of plague in London, and subsequently enclosed Richmond Park and introduced a population of red and fallow deer, so that he could amuse himself by hunting them. Charles was executed in 1649 under orders of the Commonwealth, who unceremoniously sold off Richmond Palace, which was soon demolished.

However, the park remains, as do Charles' walls (much rebuilt over the centuries) and a thriving population of red and fallow deer. In the absence of royal deer hunts their population has to be controlled by other means, and there is a cull every winter. Look out for warning signs on the gates when the cull is taking place (usually at night), and also keep a sharp watch out during the rutting season from September to November, when frisky stags can accidentally involve humans in their courtship fights. The rest of the year the deer should cause you few problems, though you are advised not to approach them too closely.

As you enter the park, take the first track on your left, thus escaping the road. Take the right-hand fork immediately afterwards and follow this narrow path, crossing various wider ones. At the next fork, keep right past a clump of majestic oak trees and continue towards Conduit Wood. As you enter the wood, you'll see a bunker on your right, which looks as if it should be home to a family of hobbits or wombles. Keep on the path through the trees, turning right over a tiny stream (or conduit). When you emerge at a clearing with a pond, keep straight on, past fenced enclosures on your right. By now the park feels very peaceful, but listen out for the shrieking ring-necked parakeets, originally native to southern Asia but which have become established in south-west London after escaping from aviaries (or, according to legend, from the Shepperton film set of *The African Queen* in 1951).

When you reach a tarmac road, turn left along it – you'll soon pass Holly Lodge, where the park superintendent is based. Just beyond are some gates, which you are forbidden to enter; instead, turn right off the road and follow the path past the riding school and through more trees. Ahead of you before long is another wooded enclosure, Two Storm Wood; at the gate, open the catch (it should be unlocked) and walk straight in. Wander along through the trees – especially pleasant on a hot day – until after a few hundred yards you reach another gate. Exit and turn right towards the road, which you should then cross; keep straight on, following the path as it veers right along the edge of another wood and meets a broad grassy bridleway. To your left you will see White Lodge, once George I's hunting lodge but now for many years the home of the Royal Ballet School.

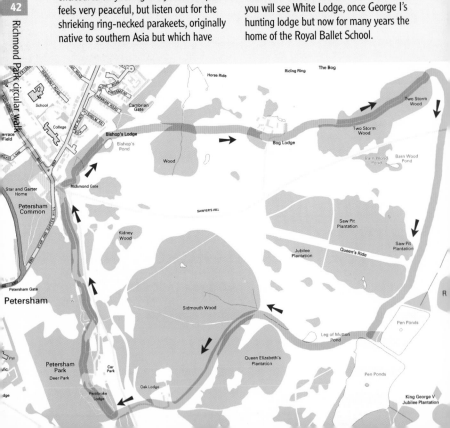

Native to Asia, this flock of ring-necked parakeets lives in Richmond.

Cross the bridleway and keep on towards the sparkling water ahead. This is Pen Ponds, two pretty lakes in the centre of the park. Keep on the broad path, passing the first pond on the left. At the junction between the ponds take the path that leads half-right through bracken, soon passing the Leg o' Mutton pond on your right. Fork right just beyond it, with clumps of bracken on either side and another wood (Queen Elizabeth's Plantation) on your left. Fork right again towards an enclosed wood (this is Sidmouth Wood, kept mostly inaccessible to protect the plants and wildlife) and follow the sandy track left around it; note the really magnificent hollow tree on your left. (Some of the oak trees in the park are more than 400 years old, and were growing here in Elizabeth I's time, before the park was even enclosed.)

When the path joins a tarmac road keep straight on, crossing the bigger road ahead. Turn right alongside the road towards the car park, then through the gate on your left into the gardens of Pembroke Lodge, a gorgeous sprawling Georgian house built for the Countess of Pembroke, a favourite of George III. It now houses a superior café and beautiful terraced gardens with a view down across the Thames. Most memorable of all, however, is the vista from King Henry's Mound, which you'll find if you continue through the gardens behind the house. If you stand on top of this large artificial mound – possibly once a Neolithic barrow and named after Henry VIII – and look north-east through the keyhole-shaped gap in the trees (a telescope is helpfully provided), you can see St Paul's Cathedral more than 10 miles (16 km) away, shimmering in the distance like the Taj Mahal. This unforgettable view was constructed deliberately in 1710, and is now protected by an Act of Parliament.

From King Henry's Mound, follow the path through Poet's Corner, which is home to a memorial to James Thomson (1700–48), author of *The Seasons* and 'Rule Britannia', and, more excitingly, to a musical bench engraved 'Reasons to be Cheerful' and commemorating musician Ian Dury; if you plug headphones into the bench you should be able to listen to some of Dury's songs, powered by solar panels. The path then leads out through a gate and runs parallel to the road until you shortly find yourself back at Richmond Gate.

The Royal Thames

London has been England's largest city and most important trading centre since at least the 10th century, and for most of the subsequent millennium the Thames was London's main transport artery, much easier to navigate than the cramped, muddy lanes on dry land. So it is only natural that English monarchs should have established their palaces and fortresses on its shores, and taken to the river to travel between them. Royal associations with the Thames date back all the way to Alfred the Great, who resettled the southern part of the city in about 886; the dock at Queenhithe was in use during his reign. The action then moved upriver to Kingston, which takes its name from its royal roots. Seven Saxon kings were crowned here, from Alfred's son Edward the Elder in 900 to Ethelred the Unready in 978. The Coronation Stone thought to have been used still survives and is visible outside the Guildhall.

It was under Edward the Confessor that the English monarchy established itself in Westminster, which became the main London residence for English monarchs for the next five centuries. Edward commissioned the first Westminster Abbey in the 1050s, and also built a palace nearby on what was then Thorney Island, an eyot in the Thames now thoroughly incorporated into the north bank. When William the Conqueror came to power in 1066 he ordered the construction of the Tower (and of Windsor Castle, a day's journey upriver), and under his son William Rufus was built Westminster Hall, then the largest hall in Europe and still spectacularly imposing.

only the highway via which the Tudor monarchs travelled from one palace to another, it also gave them an opportunity to display themselves and the rich trappings of their court to their subjects. Anne Boleyn, Henry VIII's second wife, was rowed from Greenwich to the Tower before her coronation in June 1533, at the head of a flotilla of barges said to be 4 miles long; three years later she was borne along the same route, this time to be beheaded on Tower Green. Her daughter Elizabeth I died at Richmond Palace in 1603 and was carried downriver to Whitehall for burial in Westminster Abbey.

The Thames played a significant role for later rulers, too; Kingston and Brentford both saw fighting in 1642 between Royalists and Parliamentarians during the Civil War, though London itself remained under Parliamentarian control throughout. In 1662, two years after the restoration of the monarchy, Charles II and his wife Queen Catherine led a triumphant progress from Hampton Court to Whitehall, accompanied (the diarist John Evelyn recorded) by 'innumerable boats and vessels, dressed and adorned with all imaginable pomp'. The tradition continued, and in 1717 Handel's *Water Music* was premiered actually in a boat on the Thames, with King George I in the royal barge alongside; apparently the king enjoyed the experience so much he made the musicians repeat the entire composition twice over.

Improved road and railway transport, and the increasing pollution of the river, reduced its role in royal affairs; in 1858 Queen Victoria and Prince Albert set out on a pleasure cruise on the Thames, only to be driven back within minutes by the horrible stench. But the royal Thames has not quite been forgotten: for Queen Elizabeth II's Diamond Jubilee in 2012 a triumphal river pageant was planned, with a thousand vessels processing downriver from Putney Bridge to Tower Bridge, and a crowd of onlookers every bit as enthusiastic as their forebears five centuries before.

Subsequent kings followed the pattern: Edward I moved his court to Sheen (the palace was pulled down in 1395 by Richard II, consumed with grief after the death of his wife, Anne) and Edward III built a manor house in Bermondsey, of which the foundations can still be seen.

However, the Thames reached the pinnacle of royal glory under the Tudors, whose reigns were centred on three great palaces on its banks: Richmond, built by Henry VII in about 1501 on the site of the old palace at Sheen, and favourite residence of Elizabeth I; Greenwich, the birthplace of Henry VIII, Mary I and Elizabeth I; and, most famously, Hampton Court, designed as the grandiose seat of Cardinal Wolsey, Henry VIII's chief minister, who was forced to hand it over to the king when he fell from favour in 1528. The Thames was not

3 Kew Bridge to Putney Bridge

NORTH BANK: Kew Bridge to Putney Bridge 6¾ miles/10.8 km (Kew Bridge to Hammersmith 4 miles/6.4 km, Hammersmith to Putney Bridge 2¾ miles/4.4 km)

SOUTH BANK: Kew Bridge to Putney Bridge 5¾ miles/9.25 km (Kew Bridge to Barnes 4 miles/6.4 km, Barnes to Putney Bridge 1¾ miles/2.8 km)

WARNING: This stretch of the path is prone to flooding at high tide. Check www.tidetimes.org.uk before you set out and take the alternative route described here if necessary.

North Bank

From Kew Bridge railway station, turn right along the main road, then cross over at the lights and follow the slipway down to the riverside.

Kew Bridge, built in 1903 to replace a much narrower 18th-century predecessor, is a plain but handsome granite affair with shields bearing the arms of Middlesex and Surrey, the two counties then occupying the north and south sides of the river respectively. Walk under the arches and then round on to the road (evocatively named Strand on the Green), passing through a

Kew Bridge, showing the Middlesex arms: three seaxes, an Anglo-Saxon weapon.

small garden with benches looking out on to the river. The path returns briefly to the road; turn right into the next garden and continue along the river, soon passing the appealing Bell and Crown pub. Note that the path here is entirely covered by water at high tide – a dramatic sight, but also rather alarming if you're not expecting it. Be ready to beat a swift retreat if necessary; Thames Road runs inland parallel with the path and can be reached through any of the alleys on your left.

You now pass a fine row of riverside villas, including Prospect House with its curved balcony at first-floor level, and a little further on a brick house bearing a plaque to the painter Johann Zoffany, who lived here between 1790 and his death in 1810, and frequently used the Thames as a background for his paintings.

Further on is the Dutch House, with gables and shutters in the Dutch style, and, after a modern development, Tunnel Cottage, a lovely rambling white house from 1752, with the eponymous tunnel running under it to the riverside. Just beyond it is the City Barge pub, dating back to 1484, whose terrace affords an idyllic view of the river.

Johann Zoffany's The Sharp Family (1779–81) portrays the Sharp clan putting on an ambitious musical entertainment on their barge the Apollo, here seen passing Fulham Old Church a little further downriver.

South Bank

From Kew Bridge railway station, follow the directions on the opposite page and cross over the bridge. From Kew Gardens underground station, take the exit for Kew Gardens, which brings you out into a pedestrianised square. Take the right-hand fork ahead, Station Approach, then keep ahead into Kew Gardens Road. At the end of the road turn right down Kew Road, which eventually takes you up to the bridge, from which steps lead down to the river.

This is one of the greenest and most beautiful lengths of the Thames Path, with no irritating diversions. Just after Kew Bridge the path passes Kew Pier, from which boats

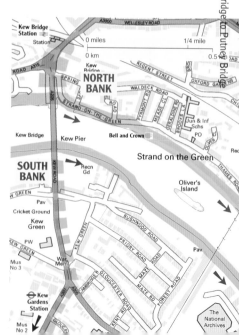

The river path now goes under Kew Railway Bridge, opened in 1869 and noticeable for its green cast-iron latticework. Just beyond it is the Bull's Head, where according to legend Oliver Cromwell escaped from Royalist troops during the Civil War, through a tunnel leading to the small wooded island in the river now known as Oliver's Ait.

This section is a lovely peaceful promenade past delightful 18th-century houses. A little further on, after a pink granite drinking fountain from 1880, the path leaves the river to follow Grove Park Road. (Soon a cast-iron gate on your right leads back to Redcliffe Gardens Riverside Walk, but note that there is no through path here.) Keep right at the roundabout and past the University of London Boathouse, following which you will pass Redcliffe Gardens itself, an exclusive 19th-century housing estate, and Hartington Court, an Art Deco block of 1938. There is now quite a long stretch away from the river, past some rather over-elaborate Edwardian villas, and a run of characterless modern developments; turn right through the last of them, Chiswick Quay, to return to the river.

Ahead is Chiswick Bridge, but there is another diversion before you reach it. Cross over the lock gates at the entrance to Chiswick Quay Marina, then left down the narrow path round the edge of the lock and right alongside a hedge to Ibis Lane. Turn left down the lane, away from the river. At the gate at the end turn right along the road and past the sports fields, then right up the bridge approach. A flight of steps leads down from the bridge; cross under the bridge and pass through the Tideway

Scullers School yard. Turn right down the lane beyond, which swiftly takes you back to the river.

You are now entering Duke's Meadow, the centre of the Thames leisure industry. On a fine day, dozens of boats are visible, being manoeuvred with varying degrees of skill as coaches bark out orders through megaphones.

depart for Richmond, Hampton Court and Westminster. The following stretch is pleasantly countrified, along an unmade track with trees and flowering bushes on both sides, which at points join up to form a canopy overhead. Pass under Kew Railway Bridge (admiring its whimsical but charming Romanesque arch flanked by Corinthian columns) and on your right you will see a small woodland nature reserve managed to protect the rare but magnificently named Two-Lipped Door Snail. Continue along the wooded path, which comes out by the Putney Town Rowing Club boathouse, after which come the grounds of Hammersmith New Cemetery.

Chiswick Bridge lies ahead, an elegant structure of 1933, made of concrete but faced with Portland stone and harking back in style to the 18th-century bridges. Pass underneath it (the squat square columns assort oddly with the elegant balustrade) to

continue along the river. The path soon joins a quiet road; you're now entering Mortlake, as evidenced by the motley but pleasing collection of houses on your right. Beyond them is The Ship pub, which has a spacious traditional interior and lots of outside seating.

The road now turns inland, but continue straight on along the cobbled riverside path past an enormous brewery complex, whose history stretches back more than 200 years; after many years as Watney's it is now owned by Budweiser. The path continues uninterrupted along the riverside, with a mix of houses on your right beyond the boundary wall and the green spaces of Duke's Meadow on the other side of the water. (If you're driven off it by the high tide, you'll need to follow the parallel Mortlake High Street.) Coming towards Barnes Bridge, the path narrows, with flats on your right and the White Hart pub, and then joins the main road.

This path takes you almost all the way to Barnes Bridge; just before the bridge, turn left through the yard in front of Chiswick Boathouse and right down a lane that feels unexpectedly rural. On your right opposite Chiswick Rugby Football Club is the entrance to Dukes Hollow Nature Reserve, a deep, wooded dell that is worth a quick scrambled detour if you're in the mood, especially in the spring when the woodland birds are singing.

Continue along the lane, which turns right at the end to pass under the charming, single-arched Barnes Railway Bridge. On the other side, turn right past the Riverside Club. A couple of hundred yards further on the road bends left; keep straight on along a footpath, turning left when you reach the river to cross in front of a boathouse. The path continues for half a mile or so under trees, many of them weeping willows trailing their boughs in the water, then past bandstands and an elegant balustrade. A short wooded section

follows, after which the path becomes more urban at Thames Crescent, when you return to a paved promenade in front of modern flats. (From Chiswick Pier, you can turn inland up Corney Reach Way to admire Chiswick House, a gorgeous Palladian villa built by the third Earl of Burlington in the early 18th century and now owned by English Heritage, which deserves not so much a detour as an entire afternoon.)

The path continues onwards for a few hundred yards, with a mix of old and new housing on your left and the wooded purlieus of Barnes across the river on your right, then turns inland to give you a view of St Nicholas, Chiswick. The church is well worth a brief detour – Perpendicular in style with a fine vaulted porch and the characteristic crenellated stone tower with narrow buttresses whose like you will encounter many times along the Thames. In the churchyard is the monumental tomb of the artist and satirist William Hogarth, who lived nearby.

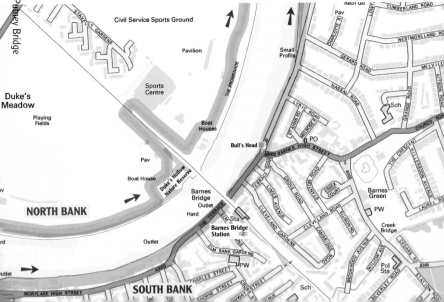

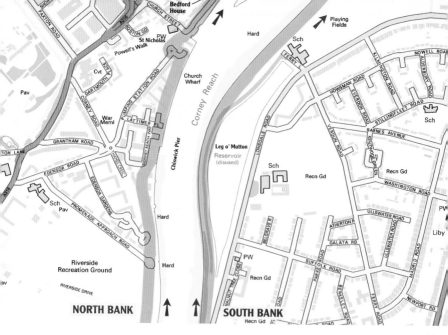

This stretch of the river is very much the Thames at leisure, with joggers on all sides and rowers shooting past at regular intervals. The path takes you through Barnes town centre, past a cheerful parade of 19th-century terraces looking out on to the river, with blue plaques marking the homes of composer Gustav Holst and ballerina and choreographer Ninette de Valois. There are various eating and drinking places, including the Bull's Head pub, one of London's major jazz venues.

After a few hundred yards the main road diverges to the right and the path continues through a pretty wooded area. On your right, before long, is the Leg o' Mutton, a former reservoir saved from developers in the 1950s and turned into a delightful local nature reserve; the entrance itself is a few hundred yards further on. Particularly beautiful in spring, when the trees surrounding the lake are covered in sweet-smelling blossom, it is home to three species of bat, stag beetles and various butterflies, as well as the many birds you'll see – the herons and cormorants particularly appreciate the floating rafts spread across the water's surface. It takes 20 minutes or so to walk round the lake, and makes a pleasant diversion from the main path.

Swans swim down a flooded Chiswick Mall: a warning to all walkers!

The path continues along a quiet road parallel to the river, past some lovely 18th-century houses from Chiswick's days as an exclusive riverside village. Most notable is the plain but deeply elegant Bedford House, dating originally from the mid-17th century but substantially rebuilt a century later. Beyond it on your left, as the lane joins a slightly wider road, is Fuller's Griffin Brewery, built in 1845 on a site where beer has been brewed for more than 350 years, and which can be visited on a pre-booked tour. Rather charmingly, the houses along this stretch are separated from their riverside gardens by the road, which is liable to flooding.

On your right is Chiswick Eyot and on your left, before long, Walpole House, originally Tudor but redeveloped in the 17th and 18th centuries – partly by Barbara Villiers, Duchess of Cleveland and mistress of Charles II, who bought it in 1700. The Walpole in question was not Horace of Strawberry Hill fame, but his cousin Thomas, who lived here between 1798 and 1803. The house later became a school – amongst whose pupils was William Makepeace Thackeray, who used it as the model for Miss Pinkerton's Academy in Vanity Fair.

The path soon leaves the river along Chiswick Mall, and the houses become a little more everyday. A couple of hundred yards on is a terrace of warehouse-style houses to your right; note the blue plaque to Sir Alan Herbert – also known as A. P. Herbert, one of the great Thames writers and an early advocate of the Thames Path. The Black Lion, at the end of the road, is a handsome, rambling old pub, very snug in winter, with lots of decent ales and hearty food. Just before it the path turns to the river again past a row of arches, the remains of Hammersmith Pumping Station. A fine view of Hammersmith Bridge opens up before you.

Keeping along the river, you pass the Old Ship pub, then soon afterwards the grand Linden House, now the home of the Corinthian Sailing Club. Before long a brick wall on your right blocks your view of the Thames; as the wall ends you'll see on your left the little-known but delightful Kelmscott House Museum, home to the William Morris Society. Morris lived here from 1878 to his death in 1896, naming it after Kelmscott Manor, the house he rented in Gloucestershire, which also lay on the Thames, enabling Morris to travel by boat between the two. Here also he founded the Kelmscott Press, a publishing venture set up to recreate the beauty and attention to detail seen in early printed books. His printing press and various other Morris memorabilia are on show in the museum, which is open on Thursday and Saturday afternoons. Just after it, turn left past The Dove (the nicest and oldest pub in the area, with a lovely riverside terrace) into Furnivall Gardens, built on the site of a Quaker meeting house destroyed by the Blitz, and then continue along the river past pubs and grand mansion blocks up to Hammersmith Bridge.

For Hammersmith underground station, take the steps up to the bridge and continue along Hammersmith Bridge Road, which passes underneath Hammersmith Flyover. At the junction, turn left down Queen Charlotte Street for the underground and bus station.

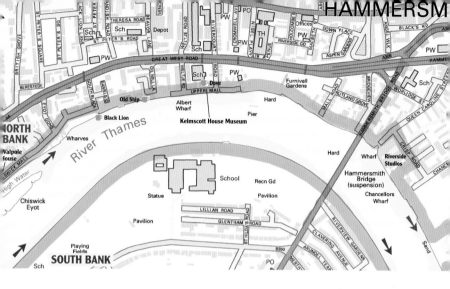

Hammersmith Bridge, a riot of green and gold.

Back by the river, you can wander along listening to the seagulls on one side and the songbirds on the other. Soon you pass St Paul's School, one of the most prestigious educational establishments in the country, which moved away from St Paul's Cathedral in 1884 and to Barnes in 1968. As the river bends round, ahead you will see Hammersmith Bridge, a spectacular green suspension affair built in 1887 and designed by the great engineer Joseph Bazalgette. Of all the bridges across the Thames, this is the most ornate, with towers of wrought iron clad in ornamental cast iron and picked out in gold.

A little further beyond the bridge, after some handsome red-brick flats, you will find Harrods Furniture Depository, another monument to exuberant late Victorian taste. Built to house furniture that was too big for the store itself, it is constructed of red brick and terracotta in a demented Baroque style, with each wing topped with pillared cupolas. Unsurprisingly, it has now been converted into luxury flats.

Having passed under the bridge, you will soon see a little riverside garden with benches, following which the path turns inland past the Queen Caroline estate (named after the wife of George II, who lived for many years by the river in Kew) and right down Crisp Road. Ignore River Terrace to your right and take the next turn right after the Riverside Studios (which has an excellent café-bar). Back by the Thames, the path continues along a paved promenade, with (at the time of writing) a brief diversion around a site designated for Hammersmith Embankment Business Park. From here the Harrods Furniture Depository on the other side of the river looks even grander than it does at close quarters. On your left opposite it are flats with jutting balconies, then soon afterwards Thames Wharf, now home to the fabled River Café, and next to it the smartly converted head offices of Rogers Stirk Harbour and Partners, the company of Richard, Lord Rogers, architect of (amongst many other buildings) the Millennium Dome (now the O2) and the Lloyds Building in the City.

Having passed a set of flats with leafy gardens, the path turns inland at the end of the promenade along a pretty street with late Victorian terraces on the left and converted warehouses on the right. Turn right just after The Crabtree pub and under the arched trellises, then left and immediately right back towards the river via Adam Walk. This is a quiet, peaceful stretch, with lots of greenery shielding the flats on your left and, a little further on, an unexpected collection of rusty pumps and other machinery by Rowberry Mead, a small local park. A few hundred yards on, past a variety of housing estates all cleverly designed to allow residents the maximum of light and river views, you will see Craven Cottage, home to Fulham Football Club. Above the gates you can spot the much-mocked statue of Michael Jackson commissioned by the club's owner, the former Harrods proprietor Mohamed Al Fayed.

Turn left inland to skirt around the football ground, then right along Stevenage Road. You can then turn

The gardens of Thames Wharf, home to the River Café, with a view of the Harrods Furniture Depository across the river.

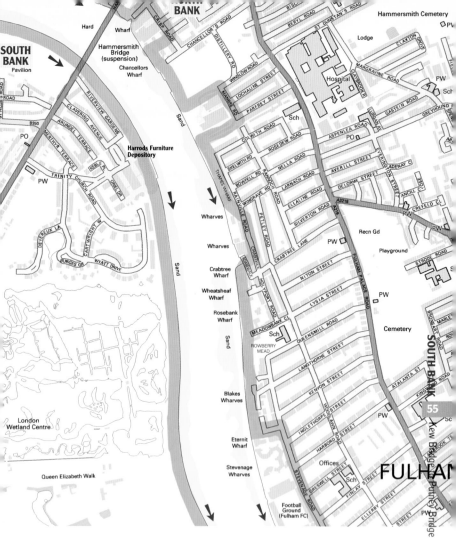

After some more blocks of flats, you will pass an obelisk dedicated to oarsman Steve Fairbairn. Behind it is the London Wetland Centre, described, not unfairly, on its website as 'the best urban wildlife site in Europe'. Carefully designed to provide habitats for hundreds of different birds, amphibians and other creatures, it offers visitors the chance to see bitterns, rare swans and black redstarts, as well as myriad other more or less exotic species. Entrance is not cheap, but it is easy to spend hours exploring the lakes, meadows and reedbeds, and the free guided tours are an easy and enjoyable way of finding out more about the wildlife in residence. A couple of hundred yards further on is a signpost with one arm pointing to the Red Lion pub, half a mile inland down Queen Elizabeth Walk; this is also the way to the Wetland Centre entrance.

The elegant early 19th-century wing of Fulham Palace, including Bishop Howley's Drawing Rooms, now a popular café.

right through the gates of Bishops Park, following the broad promenade shaded by ancient plane trees. As the name suggests, this was for many centuries the site of the Bishop of London's summer residence, and its great glory, on the other side of the boating lake currently under reconstruction is Fulham Palace, a gorgeous sprawling complex now run by the Borough of Hammersmith and Fulham and open to all.

To reach it, turn right through the entrance gate and between the two lodges – one mock-Tudor with polychromatic brickwork and a tall chimney, the other a fantasy in pink. Beyond them lie the pretty grounds, and then the palace itself – a charming melange of architectural styles from the late 15th to the 18th centuries. The interior has been thoughtfully restored, with exhibitions telling the history of the palace from earliest times, alongside stained-glass fragments, books, letters and many other remnants of bishops and their families in days gone by. There is also an art gallery space for temporary exhibitions and a lovely café in the wisteria-covered Georgian wing. The palace is open to visitors (free) on afternoons from Wednesday to Sunday, and the extensive grounds, offering many lawns to lie on and trees to lie under, are open from dawn to dusk every day.

Back by the Thames, stroll along the path – river on one side, park on the other – towards Putney Bridge. The last section of the path is a pretty formal garden, incorporating a memorial to those who fought in the International Brigade against Spanish fascism in the 1930s. On your left just before the bridge you will see All Saints Fulham, its tower a cousin of St Mary's Putney on the other side of the river.

For Putney Bridge underground station, take the underpass under the bridge and keep ahead along the lane, turning right when it joins Ranelagh Gardens.

Before long you'll pass Barn Elms boathouse, with playing fields behind (identifiable by the sound of fierce manly shouts). This was the proposed spot for one of the entrances to Thames Water's new super-sewer, but passionate opposition from local residents has persuaded the company to alter their plans and use a site in Fulham instead (see page 62). You can now see ahead a row of neat tower blocks, a sign that you are entering a more urban section of the path. Soon you will see a tributary joining the Thames – this is Beverley Brook, which wends its way through some of south-west London's greenest areas, including Richmond Park and Wimbledon Common.

The path now joins a quiet road – known just as the Embankment – which passes a small park, Leaders Gardens, and then the Wandsworth Youth River Club. You are now coming into Putney itself, past the boathouses of London's most famous schools. There is a risk of flooding here, and at high tide you may need to make a quick diversion by turning right down either Rotherwood or Glendarvon Road and then left along the Lower Richmond Road. Otherwise, keep straight on across the slipway and join the Lower Richmond Road to reach Putney Bridge.

Turn right down Putney High Street for Putney station, or cross the bridge for Putney Bridge underground station.

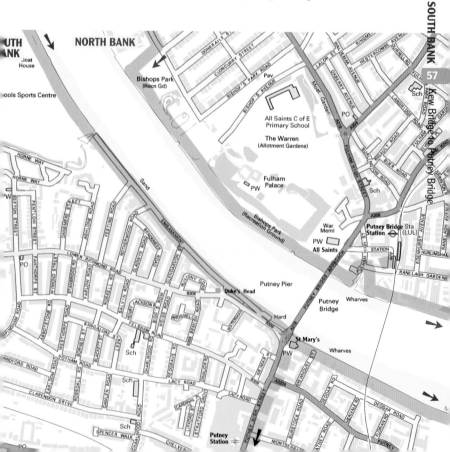

Thames Wildlife

For some hundred years, from the mid-Victorian age to the 1960s, the London Thames was black and poisonous. Described in 1957 as biologically dead, it was too foul for any fish or even insect to survive in it, and the only birds that flew near were seagulls who foraged for scraps in the sewage. Then things began to change. As a result of legislation that reduced pollution from the sewage outlets, power stations and industries lining the banks, the river started to come to life again. In 1974 a salmon was found near Teddington, the first for more than 150 years. Now the Thames has been described as the cleanest metropolitan river in the world, home to some 400 species of invertebrate and more than 100 species of fish, including smelt, flounders, mullet and eels, the traditional dish of East Londoners.

Most walkers will spot the birds first. The classic Thames species are seagulls (of course), herons, poised gravely by the side of the water, and cormorants, often seen standing on rusty platforms in the middle of the river with their wings spread out to dry. Also very familiar are mute swans, particularly in the western reaches (further up the river, between Sunbury and Abingdon, they are counted each July as part of the ancient 'swan-upping' ceremony), Canada geese and the ubiquitous mallard. But there are many other birds to be seen too: Egyptian geese, descended from escapees from captivity, terns (similar to seagulls at first glance, but more delicate and willowy) and the beautiful, though shy, great crested grebe.

There are rarer creatures too: the endangered short-snouted seahorse has been found living near Dagenham, terrapins the size of dinner plates frolic around Kingston, and water voles (like Ratty in *The Wind in the Willows*, which was set, of course, on the Berkshire stretch of the Thames) are thriving in Thamesmead. Further upriver there are otters, and very occasionally one is spotted in London too, suggesting that this beautiful and secretive animal is making a comeback. Not all wildlife is good news, however; American minks, descended from escapees from fur farms, are vicious predators of fish, birds' eggs and water voles, and the Chinese mitten crab eats fish eggs and damages embankments by burrowing.

A heron looking for dinner, in the lee of the elegant Richmond Bridge.

Cambridge (left) in the lead over Oxford, as the two crews pass Barnes in the 2007 Boat Race.

The Boat Race

The stretch of the Thames between Mortlake and Putney is perhaps known best as the course of the Oxford and Cambridge Boat Race, a fixture that has been running since 1829. Usually held on the last Saturday of March or the first of April, it has, slightly improbably, become a much-watched national and global event. Each boat is manned by eight well-muscled rowers, with a much smaller coxswain steering and setting the pace. Many crew members are hefty postgraduates, as likely to be international as British; dark rumours abound that some are admitted to the university in question on the grounds of their sporting rather than academic prowess.

The course is 4 miles 374 yards long, with Hammersmith and Barnes Bridges key staging posts. The race starts with the toss of a coin (in fact, an 1829 golden sovereign), the winner of which chooses whether to start on the Middlesex (north) or Surrey (south) side. There is nothing to choose between the two in length, but weather conditions sometimes favour one side or the other, and some crews prefer being on the inside (Surrey side) of the long Hammersmith bend.

Notable races include a tie in 1877, the sinking of both boats in 1912, and a mutiny amongst the Oxford team in 1987 which saw half the crew withdraw a few weeks before the race. At the time of writing Cambridge have won slightly more races than Oxford (80 to 76); the winning margin is usually tiny, sometimes as little as a length.

Each year, about a quarter of a million people line the banks of the Thames to watch the race, with every riverside pub rammed to the gunwales. The atmosphere and anticipation are as much fun (if not more) than the brief glimpse of the speeding boats, with the umpire's boat just behind and TV crews getting as close as they dare to the action.

4 Putney Bridge to Vauxhall Bridge

NORTH BANK: Putney Bridge to Vauxhall Bridge 6 miles/9.6 km
(Putney Bridge to Imperial Wharf 2½ miles/4 km, Imperial Wharf to
Vauxhall Bridge 3½ miles/5.6 km)

SOUTH BANK: Putney Bridge to Vauxhall Bridge 6 miles/9.6 km
(Putney Bridge to Battersea 2¼ miles/3.6 km, Battersea to Vauxhall
Bridge 3¾ miles/6 km)

North Bank

*From Putney Bridge underground station,
turn left out of the station then left down
Ranelagh Gardens.*

From the arches under Putney Bridge,
turn right into a riverside plaza and
soon afterwards left to cross over a
pedestrian bridge with salmon-pink
railings over an old dock. Ahead is
Fulham Railway Bridge, a slightly odd
construction of turquoise wrought-iron
towers and latticework (the Act of
Parliament enabling its building, in
1881, stated that the bridge must be
of 'ornamental character', in reaction
to the notoriously dour Hungerford
Bridge, by Charing Cross). Turn left just
before the bridge and walk alongside it
until you see Putney Bridge tube
station ahead, at which point turn

right under the arch along Ranelagh
Gardens. On your right you will pass
Hurlingham Court, a mansion block
with elaborate arcaded balconies and
gratuitous turrets. Beyond it is
Rivermead Court – more handsome
apartment blocks, this time from the
1930s with Art Deco influences.

Ahead your way is blocked by the
immaculately groomed and deeply
exclusive Hurlingham Club, so turn left
down Napier Avenue, a study in inter-
war semi-detached houses, then right
at the end into Hurlingham Road. On
your left you will pass the Vineyard, a
cottage dating back to the early 17th
century with a deep yellow façade, and
on your right Hurlingham Field
Cottage, a lovely Victorian house with a
slightly incongruous sandstone porch.

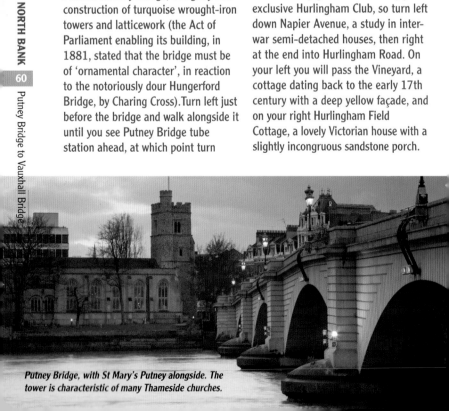

*Putney Bridge, with St Mary's Putney alongside. The
tower is characteristic of many Thameside churches.*

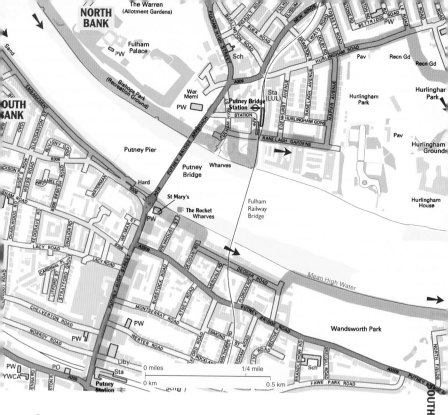

South Bank

Follow the directions from Putney Bridge underground station on the opposite page and cross over the river; alternatively you can take the mainline train to Putney station and turn right down Putney High Street to reach the river.

From Putney Bridge Road, turn into Church Square, which passes St Mary's Church, with a 15th-century tower reminiscent of that of St Mary's Lambeth (now the Garden Museum) further down the river. Its interior, however, has been totally modernised following a vicious arson attack in 1973 and subsequent rebuilding, such that the altar is in the centre of the church, surrounded by a semi-circle of chairs. The effect is disconcerting at first but rather beautiful, and the memorials on the wall bear witness to the church's history, most notably in 1647 the Putney Debates, held here after the Civil Wars, at which Oliver Cromwell, Henry Ireton and other members of the Parliamentarian New Model Army discussed England's future constitution. It is worth climbing the stairs to the gallery to admire the modern stained glass in deep colours and the light fittings, hanging from the ceiling like lanterns topped with crowns of thorns.

Beyond the church the path returns to the river, passing The Rocket and Boathouse pubs, the latter a neat adaptation of an existing building. At Alan Thornhill's statue *Motherfigure* turn right away from the river, down a short close, then left and under the pale-blue panelled railway bridge. A

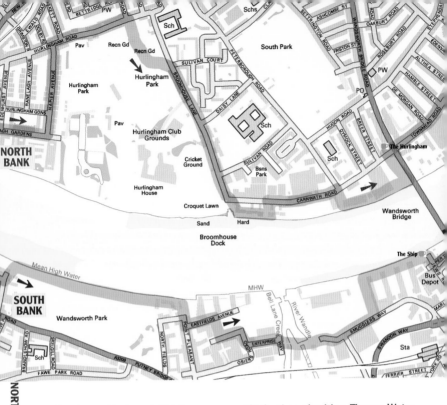

Just beyond it, turn right into Hurlingham Park. Follow the signpost across the park between the football and rugby pitches, heading for the adventure playground, and leave the park by a gate opposite Sullivan Court, turning right on to Broomhouse Lane.

After a couple of minutes you will see, quite unexpectedly, what looks like a Jacobean red-brick manor house, chimneys and all, but was actually built in the 1850s as a school and almshouse. Continuing along Broomhouse Lane, you will eventually return to the river via a nice paved walk. Continue along the riverside promenade, which benefits from unusual but comfortable wooden and concrete benches and a good view of barges being loaded up at the waste facility on the other side of the river.

(At the time of writing, Thames Water were planning to use this area as a construction site for their new super-sewer: watch out for diversions.) At the end of the promenade, turn inland to Carnwath Road, then right along a grotty industrial stretch until a signpost points you right again to the river just before a large brick building housing a joiner's merchants. Ahead is Wandsworth Bridge, painted in contrasting blues.

At the foot of the bridge, turn left along the gradually rising pathway to join the main road, then cross over at the lights just before The Hurlingham pub, and go down Townmead Road opposite. On your right is a giant Victorian warehouse complex, handsomely designed but in poor condition; at the time of writing redevelopment plans were afoot.

few hundred yards on you will see a curved archway leading into Blade Mews – pass through this and out again at the other side of the courtyard into Wandsworth Park, where you can return to the riverfront for the length of the park, along a tarmac path with trees curving overhead. As you leave it you will pass Lighterman's Walk, one of the Thames' nicest mooring sites, housing beautifully painted barges festooned with trees and bushes. Alongside it on dry land is Riverside Quarter, a pleasant open plaza with shiny new flats and a couple of restaurants.

At another statue by Alan Thornhill (this time an embracing couple entitled *Fall*), turn right in front of some striking blue and cream flats, then left at the pillarbox and right again, away from the river, between more new flats in the process of construction on your left and a perpendicular glass façade on your right. One of the path's less attractive diversions lies ahead of you: turn left, keeping the hoardings on your left, then follow the cycle signpost to Wandle Creek until you see water ahead. This is the River Wandle, after which Wandsworth is named, and which leads south to Merton and Croydon. Cross the two-part footbridge over it; the island in the middle leads to a tiny park, the Spit, from which you can stare longingly at the river. At the far side a plaque erected by the Wandsworth Society gives a nostalgic description of the mill and warehouses that once stood here. Alas, the scene today is rather less appealing, and you have no alternative but to walk on

between metal fences with the Western Riverside Waste Authority on the left and an electricity sub-station on the right.

Keeping along the evocatively named Smugglers Way, with B&Q on your right, you are eventually allowed to turn left and return to the river down Waterside Path. A riverside plaza with a view of striking stepped and curved flats lies ahead; turn right at the end and then left to pass The Ship pub, which is lovely, with a spacious riverside terrace, but gets absolutely crammed at weekend lunchtimes, even in winter. Walk along Pier Terrace and up the steps at the end to reach Wandsworth Bridge. (Alternatively, for step-free access, follow the Thames Path sign right and then left to reach the foot of the bridge.)

The River Wandle meets the Thames, with the Spit on the right.

Turn sharp right at the roundabout beyond, then walk through Sainsbury's car park until you find yourself on the river again, turning left. On your right is a long concrete platform, built for industrial use and now decaying unattractively, but much appreciated by birds. Ahead you can see the tall thin BT Tower; it is actually on the north bank of the Thames, unlikely though that seems. On your left you pass various developments, culminating in the grand Imperial Wharf, which boasts its own sensory gardens, parkland and even a station, on the London Overground line.

Go underneath the arches of Battersea Railway Bridge and you reach Chelsea Harbour, built in the mid-1980s around an old dock and now full of shiny yachts (and the odd more down-to-earth houseboat). Cross over the dock, admiring the cast-iron lamp standards with their snarling supporters.

After a couple of hundred yards the path turns inland, affording a stunning view of Lots Road Power Station. Follow the hoardings across a road, then cross another access road and keep straight on down Chelsea Harbour Drive and through the gates ahead towards a miniature pagoda.

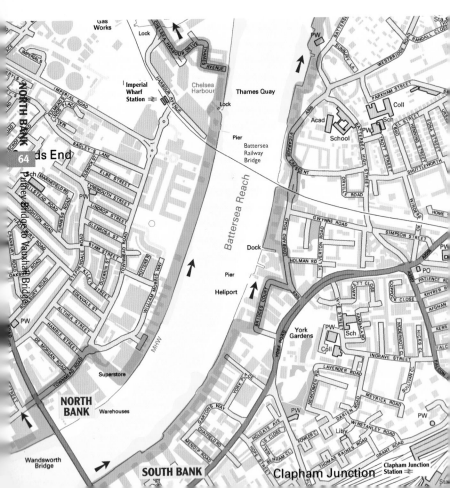

Lots Road Power Station, which supplied electricity to the London Underground network from 1904 to 2002.

Having crossed the main road leading on to the bridge (make a brief detour via the traffic lights if you value your life), you will find yourself back by the river, with a fine vista of London ahead of you. On your right is a Young's pub, The Waterfront, less atmospheric than The Ship but very capacious, with a long window frontage overlooking the river. Continue via the paved promenade, which has been sympathetically designed with beds of box and lavender, and a patch of wildflowers by the river. The residential developments ahead on your right are a superior variety, some with sweet little round balconies and then Plantation Wharf, built in warehouse style of red-brown brick with arched windows picked out in royal blue.

The path takes you alongside Bridges Wharf, between two matching apartment blocks with curved balconies. Turn right between them and then left to pass Battersea Heliport (the only one in London and therefore constantly busy) and then right down an access road and left into Lombard Road; fortunately not for long, as the path leads back to the river, below some more blue curved flats.

To leave the path here, turn right (instead of left) down Lombard Road and then left down York Road, where you will find bus routes to central and south London; for Clapham Junction station, turn right from York Road down Falcon Road.

Ahead is Battersea Railway Bridge, officially known as Cremorne Bridge; just before it the path turns right, back on to Lombard Road and under the bridge, then left back to the river. On your left is a motley collection of houseboats, and beyond them, on the other side of the river, the unmistakable towers of Lots Road Power Station on the other bank, with its elegantly detailed brick façade and its rusting roof struts open to the elements.

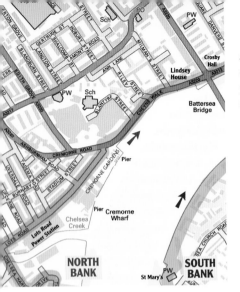

and anti-fascist Sylvia Pankhurst, and on the corner of Milman's Street you'll see a plaque dedicated to the satirist Hilaire Belloc. The road has now turned into Cheyne Walk, once the centre of artistic London – the great Thames painters J. M. W. Turner and James McNeill Whistler both lived here, and Dante Gabriel Rossetti, founder of the Pre-Raphaelite movement, spent many years at no. 16, amid a menagerie that included at different times two wombats, a llama and a toucan.

Just before the bridge, on the left side of the road and guarded by stone eagles, is Lindsey House, built in 1674 by the then Earl of Lindsey and incorporating the earlier house of the great physician Sir Theodore Mayerne, itself built on the site of Sir Thomas More's farm. Yet another blue plaque records that the engineer Marc Brunel lived here with his family, including his son Isambard Kingdom (we will meet both of them again in Rotherhithe). Right next to Battersea Bridge itself is a statue of Whistler, gazing out over his beloved river with a sketchbook in one hand and a pencil in the other.

Having passed the bridge, cross over the road to admire the spectacular Crosby Hall on your left. The core of the building dates from 1466, when it was built on Bishopsgate in the City for the wool merchant John Crosby. Threatened with demolition, in 1910 it was moved brick by brick to its current site, where it served as a student hostel until the financier Christopher Moran bought it in 1988 and constructed two new wings in meticulously recreated Tudor style.

Bear right round the side of the power station, where you cross the creek into which the power station used to discharge its warm water.

Turn right down Lots Road itself, past Chelsea Academy and the power station façade. Just beyond it is Lots Road Pumping Station, built at the same time as the power station and in a similar style, but still in use and hence in much better condition. Admire the paired round-arched windows, terracotta keystones and leafy roundels – they don't make public utility buildings like this any more. A little further on to your right is the entrance to Cremorne Gardens, which are not actually on the Thames Path itself but form a peaceful riverside spot on the site of part of the old pleasure gardens.

Just beyond Cremorne Gardens, turn right along Cremorne Road, passing a houseboat colony on your right. Across the road, at no. 120, a narrow terrace house painted duck-egg blue, is a blue plaque to the suffragette

After following the path – particularly green here, with terraced planters on your right and ivy spilling over the wall on your left – for a few hundred yards, you pass around (or through, if you prefer) the churchyard of the lovely St Mary's Battersea, built in 1775 and incorporating several impressive 17th-century monuments from its medieval predecessor. The exterior walls, in dark brick with round-headed windows, are reminiscent of warehouses of the same period that survive elsewhere on the path. The path continues past blocks of flats of varying degrees of attractiveness; note, set into the wall on the river side, a plaque commemorating Sir Roy Watts, chairman of Thames Water, who lived nearby and was found drowned in the river in April 1993.

You are now approaching Battersea Bridge, designed like Hammersmith Bridge by Joseph Balzagette. It is a handsome construction of 1885, best remembered for the beautiful gold spandrels in the corners of each span. It replaces an earlier wooden version, which appears in paintings by Turner and Whistler. The path leads up to Battersea Bridge Road, which is easily crossed. On the other side, a paved path leads back to the river, beneath a statue of a giant goose with wings outstretched.

Just beyond Battersea Bridge is an apartment complex with a long curved frontage, which houses the Hua Gallery, specialising in contemporary Chinese artists. A little further on is a dried-up inlet: this is Ransome's Dock, now known mostly as the home to the excellent restaurant of the same name. Not far from here was the climax of a minor recent tragedy. In January 2006 a 19-foot bottlenose whale swam up

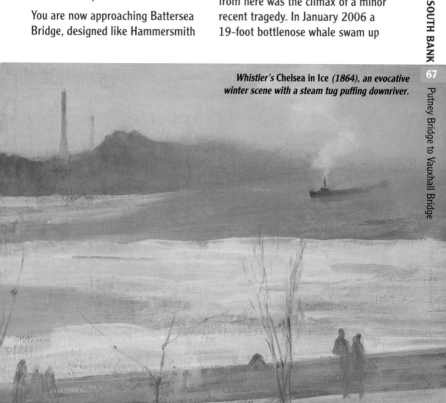

Whistler's Chelsea in Ice *(1864), an evocative winter scene with a steam tug puffing downriver.*

JAMES McNEILL WHISTLER

James McNeill Whistler (1834–1903), who was born in Massachusetts and travelled widely, but was always drawn back to the Thames.

Displayed prominently on the exterior is Moran's rather sinister coat of arms – a mythical marine creature called a sea stag bearing a trident.

Just beyond Crosby Hall is Roper's Gardens, named after Margaret Roper, the daughter of Sir (and St) Thomas More, Lord Chancellor to King Henry VIII and executed for refusing to accept Henry's newly self-proclaimed supremacy over the English Church. More built himself a house here in 1524, and his lands – he was an enthusiastic gardener – stretched from the river (where his barge was moored, ready to take him upriver to Hampton Court Palace to see the king) all the way to what is now the King's Road. Roper's Gardens are most noted now for a carving of Leda and the Swan by Jacob Epstein, who lived and worked here between 1904 and 1914.

At the far end of the gardens is Chelsea Old Church, whose origins date back to the 13th century – More and his family worshipped here – but which was virtually destroyed by bombing in the Second World War. The heavily restored exterior is of uncompromising brick, but the interior is unforgettable, jam-packed with fixtures and monuments rescued from the old church. A modest plaque to the novelist Henry James, who died nearby in 1916, is easily missed; less so the extraordinary triumphal arch to Richard Jervoise, who died in 1563 aged 27 and was clearly much lamented. Nearby is a statue of Lady Jane Cheyne, the wife of Charles Cheyne, Viscount Newhaven, and a poet and heiress in her own right, who paid for the church's reroofing in 1667. Most

remarkable of all is a dense Latin monument in the chancel, erected in 1532 by Thomas More himself, ostensibly in memory of his first wife but actually glorifying his own achievements and asking readers for prayers as his death approached.

At the east end of the churchyard is a memorial to the great physician and collector Hans Sloane, whose books, prints and curiosities became the core of the newly founded British Museum. As you return to the river, in front of the church you will see a hideous gold-faced sculpture of More, and beside the river a cast-iron monument commemorating the May 1874 opening of the Chelsea Embankment, part of Joseph Bazalgette's great scheme to sort out London's sewerage (see page 86).

A garden follows to your left, home to a pensive statue of Thomas Carlyle, the eccentric Victorian historian known as the Sage of Chelsea. You'll soon pass Albert Bridge, after which come the Chelsea Embankment Gardens, site of a

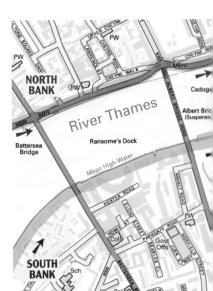

Thames Power Stations

Condemned as polluting eyesores when they were first constructed, Battersea, Bankside and Lots Road Power Stations are now some of the best-loved and most recognisable buildings on the Thames. Their river location is not a coincidence, but essential both for the delivery of coal and for the extraction of water, which was then heated to power the steam turbines.

The first power station to be built, being completed in 1904, was Lots Road, designed to supply electricity to the Metropolitan District Railway (now the District Line), which had previously been operated by steam locomotives (not ideal underground). Its external design is slightly more elaborate than that of its younger cousins, with the façade decorated with terracotta and huge flat arches, but the basic style is unmistakably similar – a great steel-framed brick monolith with soaring towers that dominate the surrounding area. Lots Road went on to supply most of the power used by the London Underground network, and (converted to use gas and oil) continued to do so until it was finally shut down in 2002. Planning permission for it to be redeveloped (predictably) as luxury flats was granted in 2006, though the subsequent recession delayed progress.

Even better loved than Lots Road is Battersea, designed by Giles Gilbert Scott, with Art Deco interior fittings and Italian marble in the turbine hall. The power station started operating in 1933, burning over a

Battersea Power Station, steaming away in the 1960s.

million tonnes of coal per year. However, its mechanisms became outdated and after some years of decline it closed down in 1983. Since then it has been owned successively by various companies, each of which has sought to redevelop the site and buildings for purposes including a theme park, a hotel and a luxury leisure complex. At the time of writing, planning permission for a biomass-fuelled power station and 3,400 new flats had been granted, only for the developers to be forced into administration. Meanwhile, Bankside, also designed by Scott in 1947, has seen its fortunes rise dramatically since the beginning of the 21st century; after many years under threat of demolition, it was converted into Tate Modern and is now one of the world's most popular art galleries.

the river, having apparently taken a wrong turn into the Thames estuary. Amid blanket media coverage, the hungry and exhausted whale was lifted on to a barge near Albert Bridge, with the aim of releasing her

out at sea. Alas, the experience proved too much for her, and the whale died the same night, to nationwide sorrow.

You're now approaching Albert Bridge Road; if you turn right you'll soon find

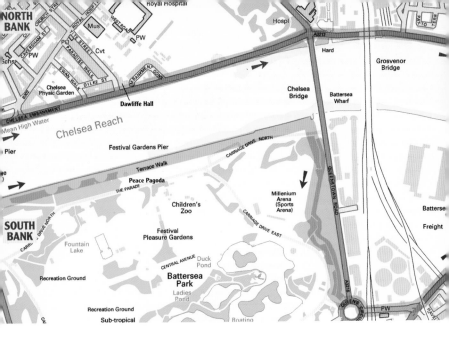

A statue of Hans Sloane in the Chelsea Physic Garden, the land for which he gave to the Society of Apothecaries.

drinking fountain commemorating Dante Gabriel Rossetti. A little further on, note Old Swan House (no. 17), designed by the great Victorian architect Norman Shaw, which cleverly employs Tudor features such as the jutting-out first floor and oriel windows. A little further on to your left is the turning into Swan Walk, from which you can enter the Chelsea Physic Garden, founded in 1673 by the Society of Apothecaries to grow medicinal herbs. Home to an impressive range of plants, it is still lovingly tended today, and open to visitors every afternoon except Monday and Saturday from April to October.

Continue along the embankment, passing various grand buildings, including Dawliffe Hall, now an educational foundation linked to the Catholic organisation Opus Dei. Most spectacular of all the buildings in this stretch is the breathtaking the Prince Albert free house, a gastropub with aspirations to be a serious restaurant. It was in fact the idea of Prince Albert, Queen Victoria's husband, to build a river crossing here, though he had died of typhoid before work started. Originally designed as a cable-stayed bridge, with the roadway supported by rods radiating out from the top of the towers, it soon proved unstable, and Joseph Bazalgette installed new suspension chains. Problems persisted (as the sign instructing troops from the nearby Chelsea Barracks to break step when crossing suggests) and in the 1950s the London County Council sought to demolish and replace it. The poet and architectural conservationist John Betjeman led a campaign to save it, which was successful, at the cost of two cylindrical concrete piers being installed under the middle space to provide support. Repainted in colourful pink, blue and green in the 1990s, Albert Bridge is now famous for being illuminated at night by 4,000 low-voltage tungsten halogen bulbs hung from its cables and towers. It reopened in December 2011 after nearly two years' strengthening work, and it is hard not to fear that it is coming to the end of its natural lifespan.

Between Albert Bridge and Chelsea Bridge the path takes you along the top edge of Battersea Park, the site of the first football game played by the rules of the newly formed Football Association in 1864, and now home to a children's zoo, boating lake and many sporting facilities. It's well worth temporarily abandoning the path to explore the attractively landscaped grounds, including a new winter garden. Sporting associations aside, the park is best known for its Peace Pagoda, situated just off the Thames Path and easily visible from the river. It was completed in 1985 by monks and nuns of the Nipponzan Myohoji Buddhist Order and is now a thriving temple attracting Buddhist followers from all over the world.

The Battersea Park Peace Pagoda, a thriving Buddhist temple and much-loved landmark.

Royal Hospital, founded in the late 17th century by Charles II for old or injured soldiers, and remarkably unchanged in both form and function. One of Christopher Wren's greatest architectural achievements, it feels like a cross between an almshouse and an Oxbridge college. Its spacious red-brick courts, with austere stone pediments in the centre of each range, form a tranquil environment and – with the myriad plaques commemorating Pensioners past and military triumphs and disasters – an unexpectedly moving one. Visitors are welcome to wander through the grounds during opening hours (10–12 and 2–4 each day), and to admire the barrel-vaulted chapel and facing Great Hall, still used daily as the hospital's dining room. The Chelsea Pensioners themselves, retired soldiers who in exchange for their army pension receive board, lodging and medical care, are immediately recognisable in their ceremonial uniform of scarlet coat and tricorne hat. In front of the hospital is a public park where the Chelsea Flower Show is staged, with a gate at the east end leading to Ranelagh Gardens, beautifully landscaped with a spectacular assortment of mature trees.

Ahead now is Chelsea Bridge, built in 1937 and notable for its pretty red suspension cables. Just to the left of the bridge across the road is the Lister Hospital, a splendid pink-brick gabled affair housing one of London's best private healthcare facilities. Beyond it is a fine Italianate tower belonging to the Western Pumping Station, built in 1875 as part of Bazalgette's grand sewerage system, then the Grosvenor Railway Bridge and a train depot. This is followed by the Churchill Gardens Estate, begun right after the Second World War and one of the more thoughtfully planned developments of the period, designed on a human scale with lots of open space.

Founder's Day at the Royal Hospital Chelsea, with the Chelsea Pensioners in full ceremonial uniform.

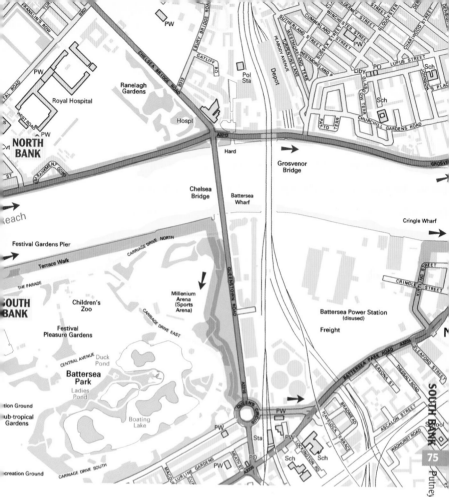

As the path approaches the foot of Chelsea Bridge, turn right up to the wrought-iron gates that form the park entrance. On their right stands a three-armed Thames Path signpost; follow the pointer to Queen's Circus Gates and Vauxhall Bridge, which leads you down through the park parallel to the main road, then down a slope, left round the tennis courts, then left and left again back up towards the road. (Note that this route is less well signposted east to west.) As you leave the park, follow signs across Queenstown Road, across a roundabout and under a railway

bridge into Prince of Wales Drive. Turning left on to Battersea Park Road you will hear frenzied barking that alerts you to the nearby Battersea Dogs' (and now Cats') Home.

At this point the river has disappeared from view, and an unexciting trudge along the main road is your fate for the next few hundred yards. When you see the entrance to New Covent Garden Market on the right, turn left into Kirtling Street and enjoy the sight of Battersea Power Station ahead of you. Crossing Cringle Street, turn right at the end of the road and you will find yourself back on the river.

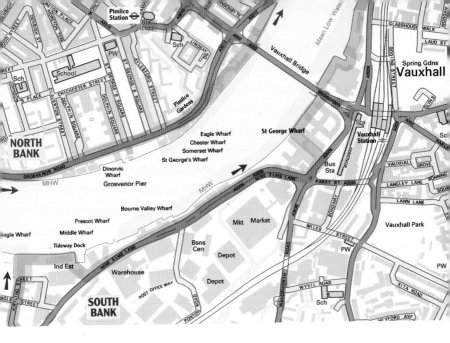

Keep along the embankment until the path turns away from the river, passing the monumental Dolphin Square, a 1930s apartment complex rather reminiscent of Italian fascist architecture of the same period. Many of its flats functioned as the pieds-à-terre for MPs, who enjoyed infamously cheap rents until the whole building was bought up by an American company a few years ago.

On your left is St George's Square, one of the largest and grandest of the many garden squares in the area, and designed by the great architect Thomas Cubitt, who transformed Pimlico from marshland to fashionable suburb in the mid-19th century. Just after the Westminster Boating Base, the path returns to the river via a small park, Pimlico Gardens, mostly notable for a grand marble statue of the politician William Huskisson as a Roman statesman; alas, poor Huskisson is

remembered now only as the first person to be killed in a railway accident – under the wheels of Stephenson's *Rocket* in 1830.

A gate at its far end opens on to a narrow riverside walkway, passing under the balconies of the flats above. When the walkway comes to an end, walk around Tyburn House, so called because below the embankment is the unassuming outflow of the River Tyburn, which gave its name to the famous London gallows which stood for centuries near what is now Marble Arch. The path then returns to the river – at low tide the remains of an old wooden pier can be seen jutting out of the foreshore – and past some boxy dark flats to the steps up to Vauxhall Bridge.

From here you can turn left up Vauxhall Bridge Road and left into Drummond Gate for Pimlico tube station, or cross the bridge for mainline railway and bus services from Vauxhall Station.

On your right is a featureless FedEx warehouse; on your left Tideway Dock, once an unloading space for coal barges and now a small and charming community of battered houseboats.

Ahead of you is the hoarding of the St George Wharf estate, which for the time being means you have to leave the river and walk down the incongruously named Nine Elms Lane. Beyond Brunswick House on your left is a flight of steps which takes you back to the riverside terrace in front of St George Wharf, with Vauxhall station on your right.

Pleasure Gardens

In the 17th and 18th centuries, before the pretty riverside villages of Chelsea and Battersea were swallowed up by the insatiable maw of urban expansion, this stretch of the Thames was best known for its pleasure gardens. Most famous was Vauxhall Gardens, opened in 1661 on land just west of where Vauxhall Bridge is now. Fashionable socialites piled into barges at Westminster and were carried upriver to a veritable smorgasbord of delights: some of the greatest musicians of the period performed here and the fancy-dress balls and masquerades were legion, with plenty of opportunity for more daring guests to slip off down the wooded avenues for a spot of illicit flirtation.

Vauxhall Gardens flourished for more than 150 years, with increasingly elaborate entertainments — in 1814 a sea battle was enacted, with firing cannons and burning ships sinking amidst clouds of smoke — but tastes changed, the proprietors did not move with the times, and the gardens became more and more dingy and disreputable until they closed in 1859.

On the north bank of the Thames there can be found the remnants of two less successful competitors. Cremorne Gardens, in Chelsea, flourished between 1845 and 1877, until its wealthy neighbours became so irritated with the noise and bustle that its licence was not renewed; a small vestige of greenery bears witness to it. Near Chelsea Bridge was Ranelagh Gardens, opened in 1742 and famous for its grand Rococo rotunda, the venue for many concerts until it was demolished in 1805. Ranelagh Gardens still exists, having been bought by the commissioners of the neighbouring Royal Hospital Chelsea and laid out as a public park in 1860.

Vauxhall Gardens in its heyday, as depicted by Maurer in 1744.

NORTH BANK: Vauxhall Bridge to Tower Bridge 4 miles/6.4 km (Vauxhall Bridge to Blackfriars Bridge 2½ miles/4 km, Blackfriars Bridge to Tower Bridge 1½ miles/2.4 km)

SOUTH BANK: Vauxhall Bridge to Tower Bridge 3¼ miles/5.2 km (Vauxhall Bridge to Blackfriars Bridge 1¾ miles/2.8 km, Blackfriars Bridge to Tower Bridge 1½ miles/2.4 km)

North Bank

From Pimlico underground station, turn right down Rampayne Street and right again down Vauxhall Bridge Road to the river. Alternatively, cross the bridge from Vauxhall station.

From Vauxhall Bridge, take the steps down to the Thames Path. You'll soon spot the bronze sculpture *Locking Piece* (1963–4); its rounded, irregular curves are unmistakably the work of Henry Moore. Across the road, on the corner of a street of handsome stucco houses, is the Morpeth Arms, a laidback traditional pub with reliably good food. Even nicer than the main bar is the Spying Room upstairs, with comfortable sofas and extensive river views.

In its basement, and visible via CCTV in the bar, are some cells remaining from the Millbank Penitentiary, the largest prison in Europe when completed in 1821, and cleverly designed in accordance with principles laid down by the philosopher Jeremy Bentham, with wings radiating from a central hexagon so that the prison officers could see into each wing from the windows in the central part. It was established as a 'model prison', whereby inmates could work and benefit from religious and moral education, but soon it became known as a gloomy, unhealthy place, with many health problems and epidemics arising from poor diet and sanitation. The capstan on the street outside would have been used by the ships on to which unhappy convicts were loaded for transportation to Australia.

Millbank Penitentiary was pulled down in 1890, and on its site was built the much more salubrious Tate Gallery, now Tate Britain, which opened in 1897 and remains one of the best art galleries in the country. Entrance to the general collection is free, the café is excellent, and you can easily nip in to admire J. M. W. Turner's *The Thames above Waterloo Bridge*, *London from Greenwich Park* and *Richmond Hill*, all beautiful evocations of London and the Thames in the early 19th century.

Back on the Thames Path, continue through the riverside gardens, with Millbank Tower (one of London's first skyscrapers, and described by A. P. Herbert in 1966 as a 'monstrous glass giraffe') rearing up on your left. Home first to the Labour Party and now to the Conservative Party, it was stormed in November 2010 by students protesting against a rise in tuition fees.

South Bank

From Vauxhall railway and underground station, walk up to the bridge and take the steps down to the Thames Path.

Just east of Vauxhall Bridge, and visible at very low tides, are six timber piles that form London's oldest identified structure. Dated to the Mesolithic Period, around 4000 BC, they pre-date by 2,500 years the remains of a Bronze Age bridge or jetty found on the other side of the modern bridge. Today's Vauxhall Bridge, opened in 1906, is a colourful structure, best known for the bronze statues on its piers that represent the arts and industry. It is sandwiched between two of 21st-century London's most striking buildings: St George Wharf, with its

stepped turquoise and white towers topped with winged penthouses, and the iconic MI6 building, designed by Terry Farrell and reminiscent of a Babylonian ziggurat. Headquarters of the Secret Intelligence Service, its ostentatiousness is particularly striking given that the organisation's existence was not officially acknowledged until 1994.

The path continues round a slipway (look out for the yellow Duck tour amphibious vehicles, which descend into the river here). Beyond it you will see the first of the cast-iron sturgeon lampstandards which will accompany your walk for the next few miles. Originally designed by George Vulliamy in 1870, they are still made today when necessary.

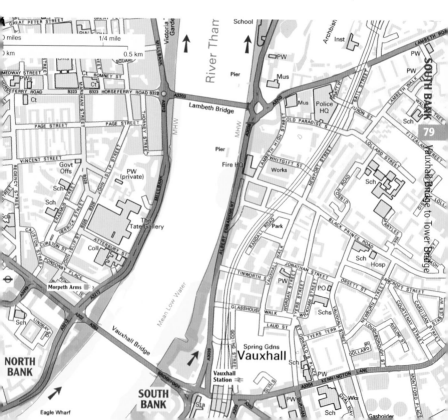

Lambeth in the 1860s, before the building of the Albert Embankment, with old Lambeth Bridge on the left.

Just south of the approach to Lambeth Bridge, and the twin to an identical office block on the other side of the entrance to the bridge, is Thames House, designed by Sir Frank Baines in 1929 and now the headquarters of MI5, the British Security Service. Although not as striking as the MI6 building on the other side of the river, it and its twin are notable examples of inter-war neoclassicism.

Continue past the bridge and into more gardens, this time the Victoria Tower Gardens, which house the Buxton Memorial Fountain, an exuberantly polychromatic neo-Gothic fancy which was built in 1865 to commemorate the abolition of the slave trade; it was commissioned by Charles Buxton MP, whose father Thomas Fowell Buxton was one of the abolitionists. Looking west down Dean Stanley Street here

you will see a lovely baroque church, in a style more reminiscent of Rome than of London. This is St John's Smith Square, built by Thomas Archer in 1728; it was brutally firebombed during the Second World War and is now one of London's prettiest concert venues. Also in the gardens you will find a cast of Auguste Rodin's *The Burghers of Calais* (1889), which depicts six civic notables who in 1347 offered up their lives to Edward III, who was besieging the city, in exchange for sparing Calais' other citizens. Ahead of you stands the Palace of Westminster, blocking the riverfront, so you should leave the park by its top-left corner, passing a statue of the suffragette leader Emmeline Pankhurst, erected provocatively and no doubt deliberately close to the seat of British government, outside which her fellow campaigners for votes for women so often protested.

The path is now running along the Albert Embankment, built in the late 1860s as part of Bazalgette's masterplan (see page 86). On your right is the road of the same name; it is rather noisy, and the buildings on your right thoroughly unattractive, but the spectacular view ahead, of the Houses of Parliament and London Eye, more than makes up for it. Before long you'll see on your left the Tamesis Dock, an old riverboat now converted into a pub. To your right, on the other side of the road, is is White Hart Dock, which after many years of neglect was revitalised in 2009 with sculptures in the shape of upturned boats, made (appropriately) from English oak. Look down Black Prince Road for a glimpse of the former Royal Doulton Factory, an extraordinarily ornate building of 1878, built from dark-red brick with eye-strainingly copious decorations.

Ahead is Lambeth Bridge, built in 1932; its red trimmings were chosen to reflect the colour of the House of Lords benches. Keep on the path as it approaches and then passes the bridge. Just after it, you'll see on your right the former parish church of St Mary at Lambeth, originally dating from the 1370s. In its churchyard are buried the family of John Tradescant, Charles I's gardener, and the building is now home to the Garden Museum, renowned for its quirky exhibitions and popular vegetarian café. The pineapples mounted on the obelisks at either end of Lambeth Bridge are a tribute to Tradescant's son, another John, who reputedly grew the first British pineapple.

Right next to it is Lambeth Palace, one of the architectural glories of the city and still used for the purpose for which it was built, as the London residence of the Archbishops of Canterbury. From the Thames Path there is an excellent view of the dark-red brick gatehouse, built by Cardinal John Morton in 1495, and the glorious 17th-century Great Hall, now used as the library. The Palace is one of the most popular attractions of London Open House weekend every September, and is occasionally open at other times during the year.

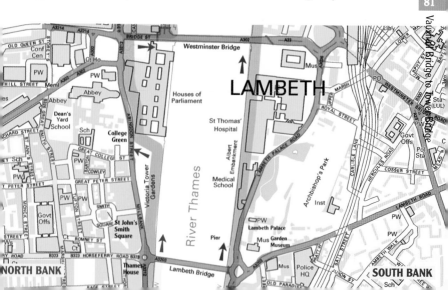

Just across the road is College Green, on which stands Henry Moore's *Knife Edge* (1962), similar in style and effect to *Locking Piece*, which you passed earlier. At the far end is the Jewel Tower, a modest but lovely 14th-century structure with round-topped windows that was originally part of the medieval Westminster Palace.

Across the road stands Westminster Abbey, built between 1245 and 1517 on the site of an earlier church. English monarchs have been crowned here since 1066 and many are buried here too, alongside many of the nation's great writers (in Poets' Corner) and other national figures such as Charles Darwin and William Gladstone. The Abbey is of course very much worth exploring as a paying visitor. Attending services is free; Evensong in particular (generally at 5 p.m. on weekdays and 3 p.m. at weekends) can border on the transcendent, and offers a tranquil respite from the frenetic crowds of tourists outside.

Alongside Westminster Abbey and rather dwarfed by it, but still worth admiring, is St Margaret's, the parish church of the Houses of Parliament since 1614 and the burial place of William Caxton (who set up England's first printing press in Westminster, in 1476) and Sir Walter Raleigh, amongst other famous names.

The Houses of Parliament themselves, stretching up to Westminster Bridge, are such a familiar and stirring sight that it's easy to forget that, compared to the other buildings in the complex, they are comparatively recent. Westminster Hall, on the west side, was built in 1097 under William II and has a spectacular hammerbeam roof; for centuries it was the heart of the English justice system, and it was here that Charles I was tried and condemned to death. For most of its lifetime it was surrounded by timber-framed medieval buildings, updated haphazardly as the need arose, but in 1834 an enormous fire broke out and most of the palace complex was burned to the ground. A public competition was held to choose the design for its successor, won by Charles Barry with his neo-Gothic fantasy in stone. Its famous clock

Palatium Archiepiscopi Cantuariensis propa Londinum, *vulgo* Lambeth House.

Lambeth Palace from the river, an engraving made by Wenceslaus Hollar in 1647.

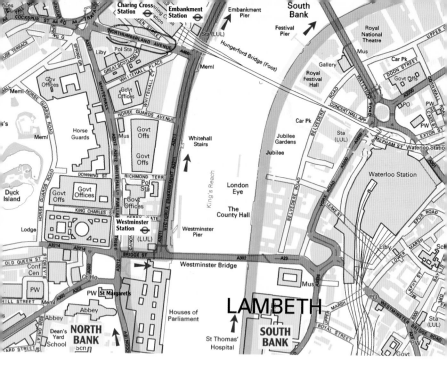

The paved promenade takes leave of the road beyond the Palace buildings, with the result that background noise levels fall dramatically. On your right now is the vast complex of St Thomas' Hospital. Founded in the 12th century, the second oldest hospital in London after St Bartholomew (Barts), it moved to this site in the 1860s, and was specifically designed for optimum sanitation and ventilation. The first you will see of it is an Italianate campanile, rising from red-brick buildings of a similar style, which in places are incongruously or just shoddily modernised. As you approach Westminster Bridge a square tower block of off-white bricks looms up, the replacement for an original pavilion destroyed in the Second World War; it is not exactly

beautiful, but much appreciated by the many patients who enjoy a view of the Big Ben clock tower from the windows beside their beds.

Westminster Bridge is no longer the edifice which Canaletto drew, and on which Wordsworth wrote his famous sonnet; it was replaced in 1862 with the current bridge, specially designed to match the new Houses of Parliament (even its green hue derives from the colour of the leather seats in the House of Commons). The oldest bridge in central London, it is beautifully decorated with Gothic quatrefoils in the spandrels of the arches and unusual three-fold light fittings above each pier. The stone lion guarding it dates back to 1837 and originally stood over the entrance arch of the old Red Lion Brewery up by Hungerford Bridge.

The Houses of Parliament, built between 1840 and 1870 and one of the defining images of London.

tower was designed by Augustus Pugin, and houses the great bell Big Ben, whose chimes are familiar from news bulletins and New Year countdowns around the world.

Continue past the Houses of Parliament; you'll note various security measures and copious police. Parliament Square, on your left, is now best known as a venue for protest; following several battles – both physical and legal – between peace activists and the authorities, at the time of writing the grassy area of the square has been cordoned off but protestors still gather around the sides.

Turn right up Bridge Street, passing Portcullis House, built in the late 1990s to provide office space for MPs; its striking chimneys, designed to echo those of the Palace of Westminster, are actually part of the natural-convection-based air-conditioning system. Back on the river, look for the statue of Queen Boudicca and her daughters driving a war chariot, recalling Boudicca's burning of London in about AD 60 as part of the Iceni tribe's rebellion against their Roman overlords.

Follow the steps down to the river and turn left along the Embankment, past the Westminster Millennium Pier. Continue along the promenade, with a splendid view of City Hall and the London Eye on the opposite bank. On the left, across the road, is the first section of the Victoria Embankment Gardens, which extend all the way east to Blackfriars Bridge. Opened in 1870, the gardens were established on the strip of land reclaimed by Joseph Bazalgette; beneath them run Bazalgette's new sewers and the Circle and District underground lines. The gardens are little changed, and offer not only leafy respite for tourists and office workers but also a fascinating array of statues of Victorian dignitaries – such as Charles Gordon, better known as Gordon of Khartoum, whose elaborate monument commemorates his noble but quite unnecessary death at the hands of Sudanese rebels in 1885.

Beyond the bridge, and stretching most of the way to Hungerford Bridge, is County Hall, built between the wars as a home for London's then governing body, the London County Council, and used for that purpose until the LCC's successor, the Greater London Council, was unceremoniously abolished in 1986. Vast and unabashedly Italianate, its most striking feature is its deep curved colonnade, the effect of which is now unforgivably marred by a hideous breeze-block structure erected in front of it. This latter forms the entrance for the London Death Trap, one of the scare-based attractions that have opened in the city in recent years, the very popular London Aquarium, home to water-loving species from seahorses to crocodiles, and the London Film

The London Eye, with County Hall on the right; as usual, the South Bank is thronged with Londoners and tourists.

Museum, which explores the history of cinema in Britain with props from films including *Superman* and *Star Wars*.

Beyond these is the London Eye, Europe's tallest Ferris wheel, which was erected only in 1999 but became almost immediately one of London's most familiar landmarks and its most popular paid tourist attraction. Its appeal is obvious – on stepping into one of the egg-shaped glass capsules, passengers are slowly lifted upwards, until the whole of London lies as if beneath their feet. On a clear day the views stretch to the very edges of the city, and a trip at night, with buildings and bridges illuminated in all directions, is equally exciting.

Bazalgette and the Embankment

London as it is today has been formed over the course of many centuries – from the Tower of London, built following the Norman Conquest in 1066, to the towering glass skyscrapers of recent years – but, more than anything else, it is a Victorian city. It was under the Victorians that most of its great civic buildings were erected or restored, that its railway network was laid out, that the hundreds of self-contained villages within 20 miles of Charing Cross were drawn into the vast spreading metropolis. And of all the gifted Victorian architects, town planners and visionaries, the most significant of all was Sir Joseph Bazalgette.

In 1848 and 1853, London was struck by horrible cholera epidemics. Thousands of Londoners died wretchedly of diarrhoea and vomiting, thought to be spread by foul air, known as 'miasma'. Although wrong (cholera is waterborne), this assumption was understandable, given that at the time the Thames was essentially an open sewer, into which the untreated waste of the city poured every day. The smell was so vile that during the hot summer of 1858 Members of Parliament considered leaving Westminster altogether, and commissioned Bazalgette, then chief engineer of the Metropolitan Board of Works, to solve the problem.

Bazalgette's scheme was ambitious and ingenious. He designed more than 2,000 miles of pipes to run under London, collecting waste from every house and sending it into vast main sewers that drained into the Thames downriver, at Beckton on the north side and Crossness on the south. The system was powered by large pumping stations at Abbey Mills and Deptford. All are splendid Italianate buildings, but the major visual legacy of Bazalgette's plan is the Embankment. Until the 1850s, the river lapped up to the buildings on both banks, as the numerous water-gates still visible on the north side of the Thames bear witness.

Bazalgette had the idea of running the sewers along the Thames foreshore, then boxing them in and roofing them over. The timing of the project was fortuitous, since it coincided with the opening of the first underground railway line in the world, which started running between Paddington and Farringdon in 1863. The Victoria Embankment provided a perfect site for another underground railway – what is now the District line, from Westminster to Blackfriars. At surface level a much-needed new road was built, and the remaining space was filled in with pretty ornamental gardens, which survive almost unchanged. It was soon followed by the Albert Embankment, from Vauxhall to Lambeth Bridge, and the Chelsea Embankment, between Battersea and Chelsea Bridges. In only 12 years, Bazalgette had created a total of 52 acres of new riverside land, established a sewerage system that is still in use today, and changed the face of London for ever.

An affectionate caricature of Sir Joseph Bazalgette published by Punch *magazine in 1883, showing the Victoria Embankment and a drainage tunnel coming out of the great engineer's head.*

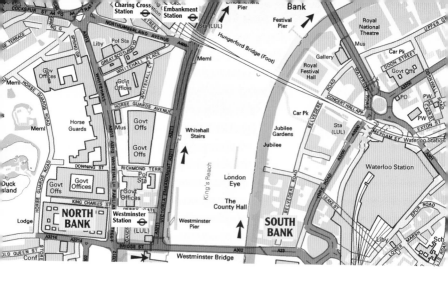

Beyond the Eye is an uninspiring plaza, usually enlivened by buskers and street artists/performers, with the Golden Jubilee Bridges at its other end. On your right is the Royal Festival Hall, built, as the name suggests, for the Festival of Britain in 1951, though the river frontage dates mostly from 1964, when the Hall was substantially refurbished. Its Modernist (International Style) exterior has always attracted as many critics as admirers, but the interior is very popular; unlike other London concert venues, its foyers are generously designed to provide lots of light and space, and the sleek auditorium itself enjoys boxes that jut directly out of the wall like opened drawers.

For many years the South Bank was rather down at heel; there was no lack of people attending plays and concerts here, but the concrete surroundings and dearth of congenial eating and drinking facilities sent them dashing off to the West End afterwards. Since 2000 this has all changed – the riverside terrace underneath the Hall now houses several of the better chain restaurants, as does the upper-level terrace adjoining the new Jubilee pedestrian bridge, and a policy of providing free entertainment in the foyer of the Hall and outside the National Theatre means that the riverside promenade is now the closest London has to the Italian *passeggiata*, a constant parade of Londoners and tourists strolling to and fro, chatting, laughing and generally enjoying everything the area has to offer.

Passing the Festival Pier, note the skateboarders zooming around the graffitied undercroft under the (unremittingly brutalist) Queen Elizabeth Hall and Hayward Gallery; this has been London's premier skateboarding venue since the 1980s, although every so often it comes under threat from developers wanting to rework the space for greater profit. Across the river, admire Embankment Place, built over Charing Cross Station, from whose gaping maw issue the trains that cross the Hungerford Railway Bridge.

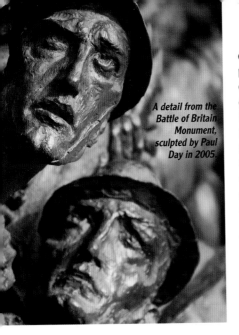

A detail from the Battle of Britain Monument, sculpted by Paul Day in 2005.

of the Embankment Gardens, where public WCs can be found. At the rear of the gardens is the elaborate water-gate of the now-demolished York House, originally the London residence of the Archbishop of York and then that of James I's favourite, George Villiers, Duke of Buckingham, during whose ownership the water-gate was constructed in 1626. It demonstrates not just how much land Bazalgette's masterplan reclaimed from the Thames, but also how lovely this stretch of the river must have once been, reminiscent of Venice with its lines of grand palaces abutting the water, and boatmen ferrying nobles from the steps of their houses towards Westminster or the City.

The riverside path here also offers a rich selection of monuments. The Battle of Britain Monument, erected as recently as 2005, remembers the 'few' who fought Germany in the skies over Britain in 1940, and a gilded eagle, wings upraised, commemorates the airmen of the First World War. Further on, past the *Tattershall Castle* (another floating bar and restaurant), is a fine monument to Joseph Bazalgette, bearing the words '*Flumini Vincula Posuit*' – literally, 'He put chains on the river'.

Ahead is Embankment tube station and the Hungerford Railway Bridge, flanked by the two broad pedestrian Golden Jubilee Bridges; erected in 2002 to commemorate 50 years of Elizabeth II's reign, they replace a dank, narrow and thoroughly unpleasant predecessor.

Continue along the pavement, passing Embankment Pier. Across the road on your left is the next section

On your left, visible above the treetops of Embankment Gardens, are two of London's most striking art deco office blocks. First is the Adelphi, built in the late 1930s in the face of much resistance, since its construction entailed the demolition of an exceptionally fine row of Georgian houses of the same name built by the Adam brothers (hence the name Adelphi, Greek for 'brothers'). It is hard not to regret this loss; but the Adelphi is a fine building in its own right, shaped like an E with strongly emphasised verticals and bronze-clad bows. The carved pattern used between the upper storeys is known as Greek key and was widely used on 1930s buildings. Next to it is Shell-Mex House from 1931, built for the oil companies Shell-Mex and BP and famous for its massive squat clock tower. It's now the home of Penguin, probably the world's most famous book publishing company.

You'll find now yourself approaching Waterloo Bridge, built in 1944 amid much controversy; its handsome Neo-classical predecessor, built by John Rennie in 1817, was much loved, but became increasingly unsafe to the point where one pier sank altogether in 1924. However, its replacement, designed of reinforced concrete by Giles Gilbert Scott of Battersea and Bankside power station fame, is also beautiful, its elegant spans forming one of the plainest but most graceful river crossings. Oddly, since the 1840s Waterloo Bridge old and new has had a reputation as a suicide spot, and in September 1978 it was the setting for the extraordinary killing of Bulgarian dissident Georgi Markov by means of a ricin pellet fired into his leg by an umbrella specially adapted by the KGB. The view from the bridge is as good as it gets, offering a glorious panorama of London from Battersea Power Station to the Gherkin.

Underneath Waterloo Bridge is a longstanding secondhand book market, and the entrance to the BFI Southbank, previously known as the National Film Theatre. On the other side is the National Theatre, built in the 1970s to a design by Denys Lasdun. Like the Festival Hall, it divides opinion, between those who see it as another concrete monolith and those who admire its complex angles and interlocking shapes, and the square tower that makes it loom over its surroundings like a riverside fortress. It houses three separate auditoriums – the Olivier, Lyttleton and Cottesloe – and remains one of the best and most important theatrical powerhouses in Britain.

Just beyond the National is the IBM Building, also designed by Lasdun and in a similar style, although using grainier concrete. Continuing along the river, under an avenue of London plane trees, you will pass Gabriel's Wharf leading off to your right – once home to a row of dilapidated garages, it's now a pretty pedestrian enclave with several good cafés, restaurants and arty shops. Just beyond are some genuine old

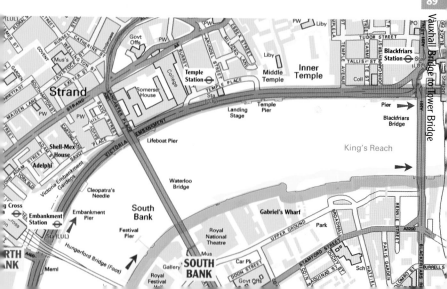

Ahead you will now see the most famous, and certainly the oldest, of Thames monuments – Cleopatra's Needle, flanked by two sphinxes. In fact, the obelisk is more than a millennium older than Cleopatra, being carved in 1450 BC on the orders of the Egyptian Pharaoh Thutmose III; the inscriptions were added a couple of centuries later to commemorate the victories of Rameses II. In 12 BC the Needle and its twin (now in New York) were moved to Alexandria and set up in the Caesareum – a temple built by Cleopatra in honour of Mark Antony, hence the name. Muhammad Ali, ruler of Sudan and Egypt, gave the Needle to Britain in 1819 in thanks for the British victories at the Battles of the Nile and Alexandria in 1801, but only in 1877 did it reach London, after an epic voyage during which the Needle nearly sank to the depths of the Bay of Biscay. The sphinxes were cast soon afterwards,

in 1882. The right-hand one and the bases of both sphinxes and the Needle bear the scars of one of the earliest air raids on London, on 4 September 1917. The monument across the road, of an angel guiding a youth and little girl, whose modesty is preserved by strategically placed foliage, was a gift from the Belgians to thank Britain for entering the First World War in response to the German invasion of their country.

Next comes the Savoy Pier; and across the road the Savoy Hotel itself, shielded in summer by the trees. The hotel, and the Savoy Theatre behind it, were built in the 1880s by Richard D'Oyly Carte, the theatrical impresario who brought together W. S. Gilbert and Arthur Sullivan, the creators of Britain's most famous comic operas. The name Savoy itself, however, has a much longer history – it derives from Peter, Count of Savoy, who was granted this area of London in 1246 and built a spectacular medieval palace here, which was destroyed in the Peasants' Revolt of 1381.

You are now at Waterloo Bridge. Having passed underneath it, look up towards your left to see Somerset House, one of the grandest neoclassical buildings in London. Built specifically as a home for government departments, learned societies and Kings College London, its construction started in 1776 but wasn't finally completed until the 1850s, the work of three successive architects who – unusually – followed the same style throughout. For many years it was best known as the place where birth, marriage and

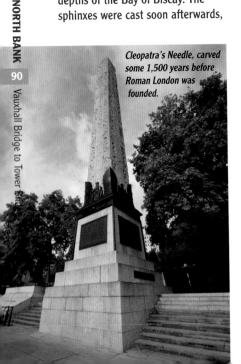

Cleopatra's Needle, carved some 1,500 years before Roman London was founded.

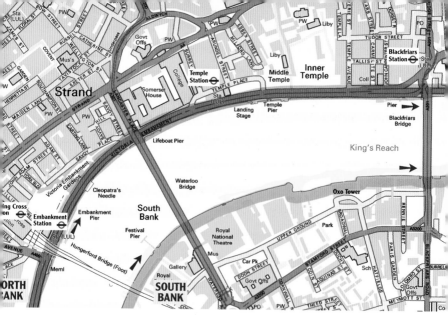

warehouses off to your right and, ahead, a large orange building that surrounds the Oxo Tower, famous for its Art Deco design and eighth-floor bar and restaurant. Follow the covered promenade in front of it, which houses more shops and cafés; immediately after it is Sea Containers House, originally intended as a luxury hotel but now housing offices.

You're now approaching Blackfriars Bridge, one of the most colourful bridges on the river, with its arches edged in a cheerful red, and pillars of a similar colour supporting semicircular recesses in a style deliberately reminiscent of pulpits, to echo the long-lost Blackfriars Church. Built in 1869 to replace a dilapidated predecessor from a century earlier, the bridge was designed by Thomas Cubitt, famous for masterminding the development of vast swathes of Belgravia and Pimlico. Blackfriars Bridge is best known today not for any architectural reason, but because

in 1982 the body of the Italian banker Roberto Calvi was found hanging from scaffolding underneath the bridge. Calvi was the chairman of Banco Ambrosiano, which (to cut a very long story short) went bankrupt following fraudulent dealings linked to the Vatican. To add even further to the intrigue, Calvi was a member of an Italian masonic lodge known as the *frati neri* – the black friars. No one has ever been convicted of his killing, which has stimulated a still-open murder inquiry and countless conspiracy theories.

Go through the underpass beneath, which is decorated with fascinating reproductions of the designs for the bridge in its various incarnations. Ahead is the Founders Arms – despite its unprepossessing exterior, this is one of the better pubs on this stretch of the river, most of which suffer from too many customers and mediocre food and service. Just after it, on your right, is the Bankside Gallery, well death certificates were kept, but in the late 1990s the Registrar General and Inland Revenue were kicked out in favour of the Courtauld Institute of Art. The main courtyard – previously used as a car park – was transformed into an attractive plaza with fountains and, in the winter, a public ice rink, and the riverside terrace was opened up to the public with a café and bar (though it is sometimes closed for private functions). The Courtauld Gallery houses an excellent art collection, particularly of Rubens and the Impressionists, and is well worth visiting if you can spare the time.

On your right is the Tower Lifeboat Station, which covers the Thames from Battersea Bridge all the way to Barking Creek, just beyond the Thames Barrier. The busiest station in the whole RNLI network, it was originally built by the Royal Humane Society to rescue would-be suicides jumping from Waterloo Bridge, and answers on average one emergency call every day, saving more than 200 lives over the last 10 years.

A little further on, across the road, is the unobtrusive Temple underground station. Behind it, stretching north towards High Holborn and east to Blackfriars Bridge, is the legal quarter of London, much of it dating back to the 18th century or earlier, and beautifully preserved (or, in many cases, immaculately restored after war damage). It's possible to slip into the Temple a little further on (the Embankment gate is open on weekdays; at weekends you'll need to enter via Tudor Street) and have a look around; make sure you admire

Temple Church, built in the 12th century for the Knights Templar, that mysterious and ever-fascinating medieval order.

Back on the Embankment, facing the entrance to Temple Reach, is a bombastic monumental arch featuring Old Father Thames on the keystone. A plaque dated May 1935 records that, to celebrate George V's Silver Jubilee, the stretch of river from London Bridge to Westminster Bridge would henceforth be known as 'King's Reach' – as it still is, though the name has never entered popular usage. Just beyond it, a pair of ugly silver dragons bearing a coat of arms of a red cross on a white background, with a sword in the top-left quadrant, bear witness to the fact that you are now entering the ancient City of London. Behind them you can see Middle Temple Hall, dating back to 1562 and sporting a magnificent hammerbeam roof; here Shakespeare's *Twelfth Night* had its first recorded performance in 1602.

Passing HMS *President*, a 1918 corvette permanently moored here and now used as an events venue, you will see on your left Sion Hall, a particularly enthusiastic late-Victorian pastiche of Tudor Gothic style, with stone crenellations, turrets and traceried windows. Beyond it is an equally vigorous neo-Renaissance stone building of the same period, bedecked with Corinthian columns and statues of English worthies; this was originally the City of London School for Boys. On the corner is Unilever House, a great neoclassical quadrant from the early 1930s, with giant Ionic columns and impressive equestrian statues.

Somerset House, one of the grandest neoclassical buildings in London and home to the Courtauld Institute of Art.

You are now approaching Blackfriars Bridge, with Blackfriars Millennium Pier on your right – make sure you stay beside the river to avoid the complicated road junction. Take the path that leads down under the bridge. Ahead, actually spanning the river, is the Blackfriars Thameslink station, opened in spring 2012 after many years of planning. Between the two bridges you will see an extraordinary row of paired scarlet columns. These are all that is left of the old London, Chatham and Dover Railway Bridge of 1864, which began to lose its *raison d'être* after the new railway bridge (also belonging to the LCDR) was built next to it in 1886, but continued in use until 1971. From the removal of the superstructure of the bridge in 1985 until the construction of the new station the pillars stood in splendid isolation.

Soon after you come out from underneath the bridge you'll pass the City of London School for Boys, one of the best private day schools in the country, which in 1986 moved to this attractive modern building from its previous site on the other side of Blackfriars Bridge. Just beyond it is the Millennium Bridge, leading to Tate Modern. A hundred yards further on, take a left turn at the signpost, past Broken Wharf House – there is no way through ahead.

Turn right along High Timber Street (the medieval street names are one of the great joys of the City, and often reflect the goods once unloaded in the vicinity), which runs parallel with the noisy Upper Thames Street. Note the solitary tower across the road, with no church attached – this

is all that remains of St Mary Somerset, rebuilt by Wren following the Great Fire of London in 1666. It lost its nave as a result not of enemy action but of demolition in 1871, when the City was losing many of its residents to the newly built suburbs and developers were pressing for more land for commercial use. Resist the temptation to turn right down Stew Lane – the name derives not from a hearty cookhouse in the vicinity but from the ferry service departing from the end of the lane to the brothels, or stews, across the river in Bankside. Instead take the next street on the right, a cobbled lane with a glorious view of the Globe Theatre on the opposite bank.

You are now at Queenhithe, the site of the only dock to survive in the City proper, and one that has been in existence since King Alfred the Great captured London in 886 from the Danes, who had occupied it for the previous 14 years, and made it habitable again. An excellent wall plaque describes Queenhithe's history and the archaeological work that has been done in the vicinity (ironically aided by the Blitz, which in destroying lots of existing buildings also revealed many remnants of London's ancient history).

Turn left under the sand-coloured colonnade (a misconceived 1980s pastiche) and follow the paved path under an even grander neo-classical portico to Southwark Bridge. Turn left down Fruiterers' Passage and then through the underpass, decorated with lovely drawings and etchings of the old City. Turn left at the other side and follow Three Cranes Walk along

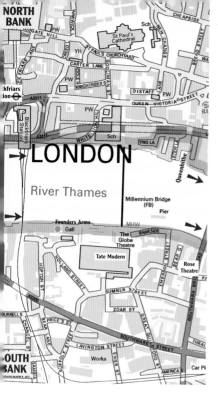

of the Tate Gallery here. Architects Herzog and de Meuron were chosen to carry out the conversion, which succeeded in retaining the key features of the existing building – notably the vast turbine hall, which houses a succession of temporary installations – while adding a glass extension on the top for a café and members' room. The collections themselves are spectacular; artists represented include Monet, Matisse, Picasso, Rothko, Lichtenstein and Warhol, amongst many, many others. Like its counterpart Tate Britain in Pimlico (to which there is a direct boat service), it is free apart from special exhibitions, and the cafés (and view from the top floor) are excellent.

The Millennium Bridge leads from Tate Modern to St Paul's, a light and airy footbridge held up by two supports that look like a pair of opened compasses. Its grand opening, in June 2000, took an embarrassing turn when it became apparent that the effect of large numbers of pedestrians crossing the bridge was to make it sway in an alarming fashion. The media, delighted as ever by a story of inadequate British design, immediately rechristened it the 'Wobbly Bridge', a nickname that took some time to fade away even after the bridge was reopened, thoroughly stabilised, in 2002. Now it is a pleasure to walk over, and opens up a splendid view of St Paul's Cathedral, itself transformed by the recent removal of three centuries of smoke and grime. City of London planning policy bans the construction of any building between St Paul's and the river that would block this view.

known for its exhibitions of prints and watercolours, and always worth a quick visit, especially as it's free.

You're now approaching Tate Modern, opened only in 2000 and already the world's most visited art gallery. The unmistakable building housing it is the old Bankside Power Station (see page 71), built (amid much opposition) to a design by Giles Gilbert Scott between 1947 and 1963. It's hard to imagine now, but for some 30 years it pumped out 10 tons of fumes a month, contributing to the horrible atmospheric pollution that plagued London for many years. After it closed down in 1981 it fell into disrepair and was on the verge of demolition when the decision was taken to house the modern collection

The Millennium Bridge, leading across the river from Tate Modern to St Paul's, is one of the most inspired recent additions to the London scene,

An 1854 view of the City from Southwark Bridge, with St Paul's looming above the riverside wharves

On your right, and easy to miss, is a serendipitous survival from the 18th century: a row of three lovely terraces. One, Cardinal's Wharf, bears a plaque which states that Sir Christopher Wren lived here during the building of St Paul's; this was not in fact the case, but the legend may have saved these houses from the fate of so many others in the area. Another, Provost's Lodging, is the residence of the Dean of Southwark Cathedral.

Beyond them is another unique building: Shakespeare's Globe, a painstakingly constructed replica of the theatre of the same name nearby on Park Street, which was built by the theatre company the Lord Chamberlain's Men, to whom William Shakespeare belonged, and destroyed by a fire in 1613. The new Globe is the brainchild of the American actor and director Sam Wanamaker, who for nearly 30 years persevered in his quest despite copious discouragement, only to die in 1993, four years before the theatre opened. It is designed to replicate its predecessor as closely as possible, with authentic timber-framing and the first thatched roof allowed in London since the Great Fire of 1666. Plays are staged here between May and October every year, with cheap tickets for the 'groundlings' who stand in front of the stage, with no protection from rain but an excellent view of the actors.

On your left past the Globe is Bankside Pier. If you turn right down Bear Gardens, between Pizza Express and The Real Greek, then left down Park Street, you'll find what is left of the Rose Theatre, built in 1587 by Shakespeare's contemporary Philip Henslowe and the venue for performances of Christopher Marlowe's *Doctor Faustus* and *The Jew of Malta*, and Shakespeare's *Henry VI Part I* and *Titus Andronicus*. The Rose is the only theatre from the period whose remains can still be seen today: its entire foundations survive, after four centuries buried under the marshy ground of the Thames riverside. It was rediscovered by Museum of London archaeologists in 1989, and a national outcry forced the developers who owned the land to allow public access to the site via the ground floor of their office block. Alas, the Rose's long-hidden masonry started to break up when exposed to the air, and the foundations were covered up again with concrete and water to preserve them temporarily. A fundraising campaign is now under way to finish the excavations and restore the entire site; do pop in (it's open every Saturday) to see the drowned theatre and an excellent exhibition, or buy a ticket for one of the plays regularly staged there.

the river. The disconcerting sound of platform announcements alerts you to Cannon Street station just ahead, the terminus for the tracks running across the irredeemably ugly Cannon Street Railway Bridge.

Ahead is, uniquely, a section of path with level-crossing barriers – these guard the only working wharf in the City, from which rubbish is taken away in barges, and are closed when it is in use. At these times you will need to make a diversion left through an underpass that becomes Bell Wharf Lane, right along Upper Thames Street, then right again down Cousin Lane. At this point the path leaves the river briefly; by The Banker pub, turn into the covered Steelyard Passage, which is redolent of the smell of chlorine from the health club next door.

Turn right at the end and continue along the paved promenade, now called Hanseatic Walk after the medieval Hanseatic trading consortium that played such an important role in northern Europe. Passing various new glass office blocks, just before London Bridge you will see Fishmongers Hall, a majestic neoclassical building dating back to 1834. The Worshipful Company of Fishmongers itself dates back much further, of course; it is fourth in the order of precedence of City livery companies, and received its royal charter in 1272.

Pass under London Bridge and across a wooden bridge over an old dock. When the path reaches a small plaza, turn left for a quick view of the gold-tipped Monument, built in the 1670s to commemorate the Great Fire of London in 1666 and the City's subsequent rebuilding; it is open daily and well worth the climb. In front of it is St Magnus the Martyr, one of Sir Christopher Wren's great post-Fire churches, whose churchyard used to form the approach to Old London Bridge. It is worth nipping in quickly if you have the chance; the church is open every day except Monday and Saturday. The entrance is from the north side, meaning that you have to circumnavigate the church to reach it; just outside the door is an ancient timber from a Roman wharf, found nearby in 1931. Make sure you admire the model of Old London Bridge in the church's narthex.

The promenade continues along the river, as you reach the beginnings of the Pool of London – the stretch of

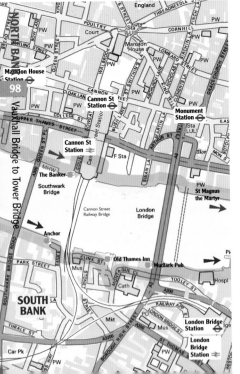

Back by the river, you'll soon come to Southwark Bridge, built in 1921 to replace a striking cast-iron predecessor. Pass under the brick arch, then in front of The Anchor, with its tempting seating area by the river, and then under Cannon Street Railway Bridge, past the Vinopolis wine experience. Ahead you'll see the Clink Prison Museum, which claims to recreate the conditions of what was perhaps the oldest gaol in England, in use from the 12th century until it was burnt down in the Gordon Riots in 1780. Past it the path leads along a narrow street with high Victorian warehouses on either side. Ahead is one of the most remarkable survivals of medieval London: the rose window and western wall of Winchester Palace, once the London residence of the Bishops of Winchester, who controlled a vast swathe of land on Bankside known as the Liberty of the Clink after the prison.

Beyond it, in a dock next to the Old Thames Inn (notable for its generous selection of ales) is the *Golden Hinde*, a full-size replica of the ship in which Francis Drake circumnavigated the globe in 1577–80, and open to visitors between 10 and 5 each day. Follow the cobbled lane round the corner to Southwark Cathedral, founded as the Augustinian priory of St Mary Overie and promoted to cathedral status in 1905. To enter the church, turn right and through the iron gates to the south entrance. (Beyond the cathedral is Borough Market, known for its top-quality fresh food and drink.)

Built originally in the 13th and 14th centuries, though significantly restored in the 19th, the cathedral is one of the earliest examples of the Gothic style in London. Much of it is restored, but sympathetically so, with a few round-headed arches remaining from the previous 12th-century church. The monuments are almost as impressive as the building itself. In the north aisle is the tomb of John Gower, Poet Laureate to Richard II and Henry IV, which has been repainted in the bright colours it would have sported when built in the early 15th century. Almost equally grand is the tomb by the high altar of Lancelot Andrewes, Bishop of Winchester and one of the translators of the King James Bible. Less impressive is the sentimental Shakespeare Monument in the south aisle, built in 1911 and partly redeemed by the relief of old Southwark behind the playwright's effigy. Shakespeare, of course, is buried in Stratford-upon-Avon, but his younger brother Edmond, who died in 1607, is buried here, remembered by a plain slab in the choir next to similar memorials for Shakespeare's fellow playwrights John Fletcher and Philip Massinger. Perhaps most moving of all the monuments in the cathedral is the plaque on the floor near the entrance to the 51 mostly youthful victims of the *Marchioness* disaster, drowned in August 1989 when the pleasure boat carrying them collided near Southwark Bridge with the dredger *Bowbelle*. This dreadful tragedy, the result of inadequate safety standards on both boats, led to a public inquiry and the setting up of four lifeboat stations along the London Thames.

Back on the path, leave the cathedral behind you on your right, passing Minerva House, a vast office complex composed of alternate brick and glass verticals. Turn right along a cobbled

London Bridge

It is hard not to be disappointed by London Bridge. Compared to the neo-Gothic joys of Tower Bridge, the brightly coloured Southwark and Vauxhall Bridges and the elegant spans of Waterloo Bridge, this utilitarian concrete structure, opened in 1973, feels forgettable and anonymous. Its lack of character is particularly striking given the lively histories of its predecessors. The first known bridge was in Roman times, probably from about AD 80; from it led a road south to the Channel ports. A later version was pulled down in 1014 by Olaf, King of Norway, who sailed up the river and wrapped ropes around the bridge's piles. As his boats sailed back downstream, the ropes dragged the piles and thus the whole bridge down – possibly the source of the children's song 'London Bridge Is Falling Down'.

Following the destruction of various subsequent wooden bridges as a result of fire or flood, a stone version was constructed at the end of the 12th century, and it was this bridge, surviving for more than six centuries, that became famous throughout Europe. Built up with houses and shops, ale-houses and a chapel in the middle, it had a gatehouse at the southern end and a drawbridge which was pulled up at curfew time each night, meaning that any Londoners hastening home after an evening outing to the Southwark theatres or bearpits had to pay a waterman to ferry them across the river. It was on this gatehouse that the severed heads of traitors were displayed, a gruesome tradition that began with the head of Scottish leader William Wallace in 1305. The bridge had nineteen small arches and several waterwheels, with the result that the tide rose faster than the water could pass under the bridge; 'shooting the bridge' involved launching one's boat over the resulting rapids, a perilous but exhilarating experience. The partial blockage of the river also meant that the Thames froze solid in particularly cold winters, enabling frost fairs to be held on the ice, with much accompanying revelry.

Alas, Old London Bridge was demolished in 1831 after becoming unstable, and was replaced a little further upstream by a handsome wide-arched bridge by John Rennie, designer of the original Waterloo and Southwark Bridges. This developed cracks in its turn, and now stands in Lake Havasu City, Arizona, having been bought, dismantled and reassembled there by the enterprising McCulloch Oil Corporation. Perhaps one day the current bridge will become outdated, and a replacement built that is worthy of its predecessors.

red
house.

S. Dunston in the east

S. Hellen

S. And'rew

the Thames between London Bridge and Rotherhithe which was the original destination for the countless ships that sailed into London from all four corners of the globe. Any cargo arriving from overseas had to be assessed at the Custom House, and by the 18th century there would be hundreds of vessels at a time moored here; the river was so congested that it was said to be possible to cross from one bank to the other simply by stepping from ship to ship. There are still many warehouses remaining from this period, particularly on the south bank; inevitably, most have now been converted into luxury flats.

Continue along the sinisterly named Dark House Walk, past an impressive modern glass office block, cleverly designed to reflect its own angles in distorted mirrors. Next comes the old Billingsgate fish market building, a handsome Italianate structure dating to 1875, with an arcaded market hall; the market itself was moved to the

Docklands in 1982. A wooden walkway (which occasionally floods at high tide – watch out) leads down in front of the Custom House. There has been a Custom House on this site since at least the 14th century; the current building, dating from the early 19th century, has an elegant long river frontage, necessary given the number of ships queuing up to land here.

Ahead is Sugar Quay Walk, pleasingly the home of sugar company Tate & Lyle, who commissioned the current rather unexciting office building in the mid-1970s. The riverside promenade here was closed at the time of writing – instead, turn left up the cobbled lane, then right down Lower Thames St, which leads up to the courtyard in front of the Tower of London, with the Tower Millennium Pier off to the right. Turn right through the entrance gates and fight your way through the crowds of tourists and back to the river. From here you have an excellent view of the Tower complex, and if you don't have the time or money to spare for a proper visit (which is certainly worth it, if the chance arises) you can get a good sense of the extraordinary mix of buildings and their history.

Immediately after the Tower is Tower Bridge, and the end of this section of the path.

Cross under the bridge and up the steps to the bridge itself. Turn inland, then left along the main road. Cross over the big road junction; Tower Gateway DLR station is ahead on your right. For Tower Hill underground station, turn left into the garden plaza; the tube station is ahead.

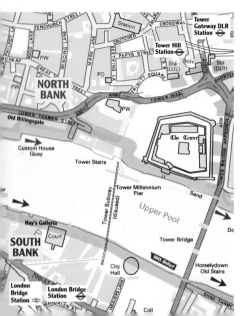

Hays Galleria, a particularly elegant covered dock now redeveloped as a shopping mall.

lane, the river visible on your left, and past The Mudlark pub – named for the children who played and scavenged on the Thames foreshore in days gone by. Walk under London Bridge, past the Mug House pub on the left and on the right the London Bridge Experience and the London Tombs. The path then passes between various offices; ahead is London Bridge Hospital, which boasts a handsome red-brick façade, built in 1903 in a 17th-century style. Turn left before you reach it to return to the river under a polished marble colonnade, turning right along The Queen's Walk.

London Bridge pier is ahead on your left; beyond it is Hay's Galleria, built in the 1850s as a covered dock surrounded by warehouses, but now filled in and an unusually light and peaceful shopping mall, enlivened by *The Navigators*, a spectacular fusion of ships and sea monster by the sculptor David Kemp. Beyond it is the Horniman at Hays, a pub whose enthusiastic internal ornamentation deliberately harks back to the Victorian age.

On the river is HMS *Belfast*, a Royal Navy cruiser launched in 1938 that played an important role in the Second World War and is now run by the Imperial War Museum as a visitor attraction. It is open daily between 10 and 6 (5 in winter) and offers a rare opportunity to imagine life at sea.

Ahead your eye will inevitably be drawn to Tower Bridge – but note the odd egg-shaped building on the right. This is City Hall, designed by Norman Foster and home to the Greater London Authority, which was established in 2000, 14 years after its predecessor, the Greater London Council, was abolished by Mrs Thatcher. On weekdays it is open to the public, and well worth a quick visit to admire the dizzying view up through the building. It is surrounded by equally high-tech blocks and a windswept plaza now known as More London.

Cross over Tower Bridge and turn left along the main road. Cross over the big road junction; Tower Gateway DLR station is ahead on your right. For Tower Hill underground station, turn left into the garden plaza; the tube station is ahead.

Tower Bridge

For hundreds of years, London's defining landmark was London Bridge – ancient, narrow and built high with shops and houses. Today even most Londoners would fail to recognise the modern London Bridge in isolation, but Tower Bridge is known and loved across the world.

By the late 19th century it was apparent that London needed a bridge at the east end of the City. After a heated public competition, construction began in 1886, finishing eight years later. Seagoing ships still regularly moored in the Pool of London just west of the bridge, and hence the lower walkway is composed of two bascules, as they are known, which can be raised to let ships through. The vast machinery required was originally powered by steam, replaced in 1974 by an electro-hydraulic system.

Unlike its elegant predecessors further upriver, Tower Bridge is gloriously, unashamedly Victorian Gothic in style, and inevitably attracted sneers from architectural purists, one of whom described it as representing 'the vice of tawdriness and pretentiousness'. Needless to say, the general public has never agreed, and the Tower Bridge exhibition is perennially popular. Accessed via the second gatehouse from the north of the bridge, it allows visitors to inspect the original mechanism powering the bascules and cross the bridge on the upper enclosed walkway. Alongside the thrill of standing 140 feet (42 metres) above ground, gazing upriver at Tate Modern and HMS *Belfast* and downriver to Canary Wharf and the Isle of Dogs, there is usually an evocative selection of archive photographs of London on show.

Tower Bridge standing above the busy Pool of London, c.1930.

The Tower of London: once a terrifying fortress, now a picture-perfect medieval castle.

The Tower of London

These days the Tower looks diminutive and charmingly olde-worlde in comparison to the hulking office blocks that surround it. However, when its construction began, in about 1078, and for many centuries afterwards, it would have dominated the entire City – a vast fortress looming over the simple, predominantly wooden houses and shops that surrounded it. This was quite deliberate on the part of its founder, William the Conqueror, who had invaded England only 12 years previously and was determined to enforce his will on an unenthusiastic populace.

The square keep, with its iconic turrets at each corner, is the White Tower, so called because for many years the exterior was whitewashed. This is the oldest and central structure in the complex, completed by 1100 though inevitably altered at various points during the subsequent 900 years. Most of the smaller towers were then built in the 13th century, under first Henry III and then Edward I. In 1235 Henry received three lions as a gift from King Louis of France; they were early members of the Tower Menagerie, which at different points included elephants, tigers and ostriches. By the 15th century the Tower's principal function was as an armoury, and it also started to be used as a gaol. In the following century, under the Tudors, numerous political prisoners were held here, and sometimes tortured; one such was Guido (Guy) Fawkes, one of the instigators of the Gunpowder Plot in 1605.

As you make your way along the river, you will pass Traitors' Gate, at the base of St Thomas's Tower, and so called because it was through this water-gate that those accused of betraying the ruling monarch were brought to be imprisoned. Behind St Thomas's Tower is the Bloody Tower; once named the Garden Tower, it gained its sinister nickname from the suspected murder there of the Princes in the Tower, the sons of Edward IV, who were kept captive here in 1483 after Edward's brother Richard III made himself king. Later the Bloody Tower was home to the great explorer Sir Walter Raleigh, who was imprisoned here for several years, during which he wrote his *Historie of the World*, until his execution in 1618.

Following the Civil Wars of 1642–60, the Tower was redeveloped as a barracks, and in the late 18th century substantial building work was carried out – this is when most of the 'infill' buildings between the towers date from. After that it progressively declined in importance, and in 1832, following several regrettable escapes, the animals of the Menagerie were moved to the new London Zoo. Now just the ravens remain – fortunately, since according to legend if the ravens ever leave the Tower the kingdom will fall.

6 Tower Bridge to Greenwich

NORTH BANK: Tower Bridge to Island Gardens 6½ miles/10.4 km
(Tower Bridge to Limehouse 2¼ miles/3.6 km, Limehouse to Island
Gardens 4¼ miles/6.8 km)

SOUTH BANK: Tower Bridge to Greenwich 5¾ miles/9.25 km (Tower
Bridge to Rotherhithe 2¼ miles/3.6 km, Rotherhithe to Greenwich
3½ miles/5.6 km)

North Bank

*From Tower Hill underground station, turn
left out of the exit and make your way
through the plaza, with the Tower of
London on your right. You'll pass a vast
stone buttress on your right – this is a
remnant of the ancient City wall, the lower
half of it Roman with medieval stonework
on top. The plaza descends gently to a
road junction, with Tower Gateway DLR
station on the other side. Take the right-
hand traffic lights over no fewer than four
crossings and into a small tree-filled
corner overlooking the Tower, then left
along the main road. At the next junction
turn right on to Tower Bridge Approach.
Just before the first gatehouse, a flight of
steps leads down to the Thames Path.*

Leaving Tower Bridge behind you,
you'll soon pass St Katharine's
Pier. Passing the vast concrete bulk
of the Tower Hotel, the path leads
you over a lock and into the old St
Katharine Docks, originally built in
the 1820s. Except for Ivory House
on the north side, most of its
warehouses were destroyed in the
war or demolished thereafter, but
the successor buildings follow the
same scale and layout, making this
an attractive and very popular
marina. The Dickens Inn, galleried
and weatherboarded, is an
architectural curiosity. Originally
built in the 18th century, it was
condemned to demolition in the
1970s when its site was chosen for
redevelopment, and saved by being
moved 75 yards (70 metres) west
and rebuilt as you see it today.

The Thames Path is, unusually,
rather coyly signposted here, with
easily missed round plaques on the
wall. Turn right from the lock,
walking between the white,
colonnaded Dockmaster's House on
your left and Devon House on your
right. Follow the paved road round
to your right – now St Katharine's
Way – and past more converted
warehouses, then turn down the

*The entrance to St Katharine
Docks, now used by yachts
and narrowboats rather than
tea clippers and spice ships.*

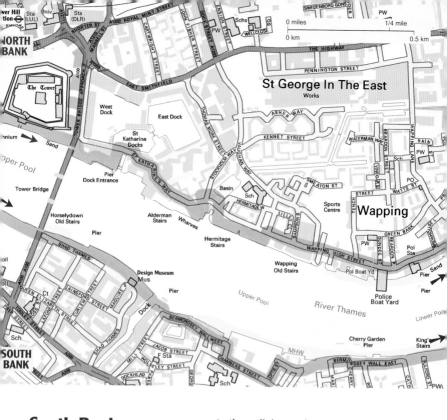

South Bank

The easiest way to join the Thames Path on the southern side is to take tube or DLR to Tower Hill/Gateway; follow the instructions on the opposite page but cross Tower Bridge rather than descending to river level. Alternatively, take the train or tube to London Bridge station (page 98) and join the Thames Path there.

Passing under Tower Bridge, continue along the cobbled street ahead; the tall warehouses further on give a good sense of what this whole area would once have been like. Turn left down Maggie Blake's Cause – a street name that sounds Dickensian but in fact commemorates a recent victory, that of a local activist who fought to allow access to the Thames river path for everyone, against developers who wanted to restrict it

to those dining at the expensive restaurants opened in the 1980s in the old warehouse buildings. Back on the river, the path leads past shops and the ever-popular Butler's Wharf Chop House, then on to a wider plaza at the Butler's Wharf pier, home to some of London's grandest passenger boats, including a replica Mississippi paddle steamer. Ahead the river opens up, with boats of all shapes and ages plying their trades or moored alongside the bank – though it's still very quiet compared to the heyday of the Port of London, when it was said one could cross the river by walking from one ship's deck to the next.

Continuing along the riverside, you'll soon reach the Design Museum,

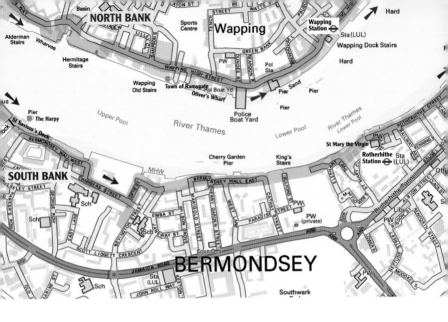

alleyway after Millers Wharf and Alderman Stairs, past an odd building with a glass upper storey and white hemispherical tower. This leads you on to a riverside plaza with a splendid vista of the post-industrial Pool of London – a melange of warehouses, flats, office blocks, working boats and pleasure boats, all framed by Tower Bridge on one side and the open river on the other. At the end of the plaza the path turns left through a gate, and then right past Riviera Court and on to Wapping High Street. Turn into the pretty Hermitage Riverside Memorial Garden, on the site of an area devastated by the terrifying firebomb raids of 29 December 1940, and now dedicated to the East London civilians killed during the Second World War.

The path continues beside blocks of flats, then left away from the river. Turn right down Wapping High Street; on your right is Wapping Pier Head, a row of gorgeous Georgian houses built for dock officials in the early 19th century and now (of course) converted into flats and leading a very quiet existence compared to their previous life of hustle and bustle. One of these houses is the old Customs House, so located because it was next to the entrance to the London Docks.

Wapping is an odd place these days, pleasant to wander through with its mix of architectural styles and quiet riverside lanes, but strangely lifeless. Continue past the inviting and spacious Town of Ramsgate pub; the building dates from 1758, replacing an earlier pub of the same name which can be traced back to 1545. Its narrow, characterful riverside terrace gives a sense of what this area used to be like, every inch of space crammed with wharfs and warehouses.

Continue along the road, passing the Tudor Gothic Oliver's Wharf, once a tea warehouse. It's worth making a housed in a former banana warehouse restyled to look like a 1930s seaside pavilion. Opened in 1989, it houses regularly changing and always engaging exhibitions reflecting all aspects of modern style, from chairs and pottery to cars and book covers. The café is excellent, with the Blueprint Café on the first floor offering more formal dining. A little further on is St Saviour's Dock, named for the Cluniac abbey that once stood here. Now immaculately preserved, in the early 19th century this was one of London's most wretched areas. Just east of the dock was Jacob's Island, which was surrounded by tidal ditches and crammed with rickety wooden houses and 'every loathsome indication of filth, rot and garbage'. Dickens set the climactic scene of *Oliver Twist* (1838) here, depicting the villainous Bill Sikes climbing up to the top of the houses in an attempt to escape, and meeting a horrible fate. The cholera epidemic of 1849 affected Jacob's Island particularly badly –

unsurprisingly, since its inhabitants' only water supply was the vilely polluted Thames – and in the early 1850s the ditches were filled in and warehouses built on top of them.

Past the entrance to The Harpy – a house mounted on a floating wooden platform, with the Downings Roads houseboat moorings behind – the path turns inland through a narrow passageway, then round a small car park and along Bermondsey Wall West, parallel to the river. The lane leads between modern flats for a few hundred yards; at the end of the road turn right down East Lane and left down Chambers Street, past tall hoardings guarding a site earmarked for the new Thames super-sewer. Turn left up Loftie Street then right along Bermondsey Wall East, and then left through Fountain Green Square, which, although architecturally indifferent, could hardly be bettered in terms of location, set as it is right on the river with a view of Oliver's Wharf and the old Customs House.

The Design Museum (right), with a fine view across the river to shiny new flats on the opposite side.

quick diversion down Scandrett Street, to the left, to admire the former St John of Wapping church and school, both in best domestic Georgian style with wonderfully over-ambitious entrances. Back on Wapping High Street, just past the characteristic gantries leading between warehouses at upper-floor level (one has been planted up as an aerial garden) is a low modernist building decorated with abstract concrete shapes; this is the Metropolitan Police boatyard, and next to it is Wapping Police Station, where the Marine Policing Unit is based. Next comes Waterside Gardens, a pleasant green space allowing a handsome view of a Georgian building – The Angel pub – across the river. The Captain Kidd pub a little further on is named after the famous pirate, hanged at Wapping's nearby Execution Dock in 1701. Execution Dock was run by the Admiralty, who only had jurisdiction over the water, so the gallows were erected with their foot below the low-water mark and the bodies of hanged criminals were left dangling until the tide had passed over them three times.

Oliver's Wharf, built in 1869–70 and boasting the most elaborate warehouse façade on the Thames.

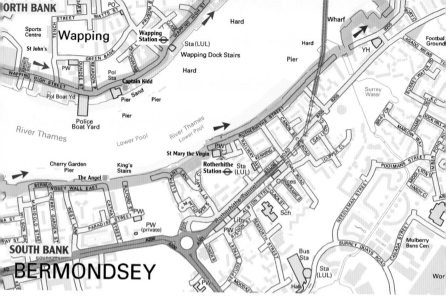

The path follows the river under an avenue of trees, seeming to turn momentarily inland before entering Cherry Gardens, which is paved rather than grassy. At Angel Wharf it rejoins Bermondsey Wall East, passing a plaza which until recently housed a statue and plaque remembering Dr Alfred Salter, who played a major role in improving this famously impoverished area in the early 20th century (alas, the statue was stolen in November 2011, presumably to be melted down as scrap metal). The grassy park on your right is home – quite unexpectedly – to the remains of a moated manor house, built for King Edward III in 1353.

Continue past The Angel pub, which dates back to the 15th century, when it was run by monks from the local priory. You're now across the Thames from Wapping River Police Station, a large white building covered in concrete shapes. On your right is a large grass mound, known as King's Stairs Gardens.

Keeping along the river, the path passes under two blocks of flats separated by a flight of river stairs and then descends some steps and continues right inland, then left to join Rotherhithe Street, a narrow lane with a few warehouses and overhead walkways – now improvised aerial gardens – remaining.

A graveyard on your right alerts you to the presence of St Mary the Virgin Rotherhithe, a dignified church rebuilt in 1715 in characteristic post-Wren style on the site of a medieval predecessor. Often only the lobby is open to visitors, but if you're allowed into the main body of the church it's worth admiring the many splendid memorial plaques that bear witness to the parish's rich history. Most famously, the *Mayflower* sailed from here to the New World in 1620 with her cargo of Puritans; three of her owners are buried here. Just across the road is the old Free School, with figures of children dressed in its

Beyond the Captain Kidd are King Henry's and Gun Wharves, then Wapping Overground station, part of the orbital railway which runs around the edge of central London. Soon afterwards the path leads right and back to the river, through a red gate which may be closed but should be kept unlocked until sunset. Continue along the riverfront, through a blue gate, and then left through a bigger blue gate away from the river. On your right is New Crane Walk, a pretty enclosed courtyard housing various small shops. A pizzeria and wine bar follow, before the path turns right, though not back to the river but along Wapping Wall, a cobblestoned street with yet more warehouses. Just as the road veers left you'll see on your right the Prospect of Whitby, the oldest and perhaps most famous of London riverside pubs, dating back to around 1520 (when it was known as the Devil's Tavern) but almost entirely rebuilt in the early 19th century with the bow windows characteristic of the period. It's worth buying a drink to enjoy the atmospheric interior and river views, not to mention the atmospheric (mock) gallows on the foreshore.

Ahead is a fearsome swingbridge guarding Shadwell Basin, and on your left the handsome though oddly shaped former Wapping Hydraulic Power Station, now an arts centre known as the Wapping Project, with a restaurant famous for its weekend brunches and surviving hydraulic machinery. Turn right away from both and past Trafalgar Court back to the river. The path now winds in front of flats, with a fine view across to the towers of Canary Wharf.

Turn inland when a dock blocks your way and then right over the swingbridge and right again down an alleyway alongside the King Edward Memorial Park. (A Thames Path signpost points straight on for an alternative route that bypasses the park and turns right up The Highway.) The riverside path passes a fine Edwardian red-brick building with cast-iron shutters bearing the LCC (London County Council) monogram – this is an access shaft to the Rotherhithe Tunnel, and has an identical twin across the river. At the time of writing this pleasant, tree-filled park, like several other sites on the Thames Path (see pages 62 and 109), was under threat from Thames Water, who seek to erect ventilation towers for their proposed super-sewer here, blocking access to the riverside path for several years.

The old school of St Mary Rotherhithe.

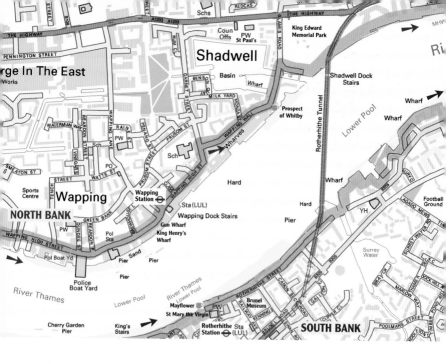

quaint uniform above the door; next to it, a rare survival, is the old watch house, from which a beadle, constable and several watchmen kept local order until the Metropolitan Police was founded in 1829.

Back on the path, you'll pass The Mayflower pub, a tempting little establishment with hearty food and a riverside terrace. Just beyond it on your right is the charmingly old-fashioned Brunel Museum, in the engine house built by Marc Brunel to house the steam-powered pumps that drained water from the Thames Tunnel, the first tunnel to be constructed underneath a major river and still in use as part of the London Overground network. The displays inside tell the tunnel's story, including the narrow escape from drowning of Brunel's son Isambard Kingdom, who in 1828 was superintending works in the tunnel when floodwaters suddenly rushed in.

If you're planning to finish for the day here, turn right outside the museum down Railway Avenue, which leads to Rotherhithe overground station.

Continue along Rotherhithe Street, turning left past Charles Hay and Son's boat repair workshop to the river promenade. Continue along the river – across the Thames the delicate spire of St Paul's Shadwell rises above the blocks of flats by Metropolitan Wharf – then up a zigzag ramp and past a large pier enlivened by a steel bird sculpture. Ahead, the handsome rounded red-brick building with stone dressings is the access shaft for the nearby Rotherhithe Tunnel, open to all when the tunnel was pedestrianised but now for emergency use only.

Take the steps down to the road and turn left over the fearsome-looking bridge and left again around the lively Old Salt Quay pub. Follow the promenade along the river, weaving

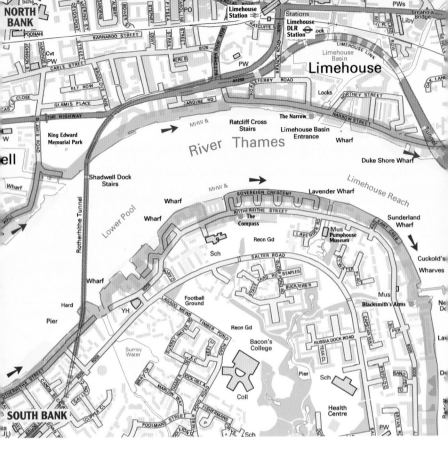

Leaving the park, pass in front of some pleasantly jumbled red-brick flats, then some hacked-about but still attractive old wharf buildings. Follow the row of silver birch trees along the river, then turn left inland and right on to Narrow Street, like Wapping High Street a mix of converted warehouses (Sun Wharf, once the home of film director David Lean, is particularly fine) and infill flats.

You're now in Limehouse, once a village where lime kilns were built and for hundreds of years a centre for shipbuilding and kitting out. More excitingly, in the 19th century the area became infamous for its opium dens, allegedly run by Chinese sailors who tricked innocent British seamen into becoming dependent on what we would now call heroin. (In fact, although opium smoking was common among the Chinese and a few Westerners experimented with it, there is little proof that these abodes of vice actually existed.)

To reach Limehouse station, turn left through the fountain plaza.

A signpost leads you right down a narrow alleyway and left along the river (those avoiding steps should stay on Narrow Street), then around the classy pub The Narrow. Take the steps back up on its other side, around docks and in front of flats of varying degrees of architectural merit, until a vast warehouse blocks your way and forces you to turn inland and left along Rotherhithe Street. At the Compass pub turn left through black gates and right along the river to enter an estate of innocuous quasi-Georgian townhouses. Across the water is the entrance to Limehouse Marina, then a little further on the stately square tower of Hawksmoor's St Anne's Limehouse.

(If you fancy a brief diversion, turn right just before the bridge over the dock and across the road to the Pumphouse Museum. Inhabiting a former pumphouse built in 1929 to regulate the water level in the Surrey Docks, it is home to the Rotherhithe Heritage Museum, which is open on weekdays and displays a collection of artefacts found on the Thames foreshore. Next to it is Lavender Pond Nature Reserve, a small but pretty man-made lake with reeds and a boardwalk on the site of the old Lavender Dock.)

Back on the path, when you reach the boundary of the estate, the glass skyscrapers of Canary Wharf rearing up ahead, follow the path around the steps and past a stone obelisk, continuing along the river as it curves right and south. If you're avoiding steps, follow the signpost right through a brick gateway and left along the main road; otherwise walk right up to the fine Canada Wharf building ahead and turn right alongside it to the road. Turn left towards the Blacksmith's Arms, then left after the Nelson Dock warehouses and up the steps, and right through the Hilton car park (if avoiding steps, use the ramp a little further on). Between the path and the road is Nelson House, a handsome 18th-century building with no connection to the great admiral of the same name.

Circumnavigate the dock ahead and continue past the health club and left back to the river. The promenade continues past flats and through the pretty wooded Durand's Wharf park;

Whistler was fascinated by the eastern reaches of the Thames; this 1878 lithotint of Limehouse in seedier days irresistibly recalls Dickens' Our Mutual Friend, *much of which is set here.*

where there is a level crossing – to guard not a railway track but a whole section of road, which swivels sideways when necessary to allow vessels to pass through the lock that functions as the gateway between the Thames and the canal system. (When the barriers are down you'll need to go up Horseferry Road and turn right for Limehouse Marina – almost entirely a modern development, but for the elegant arched railway bridge on its far side and the battered tower of Nicholas Hawksmoor's St Anne's Limehouse on the north-east corner. Walk along the river side of the marina and turn right alongside the lock, which you should be able to cross on a narrow bridge; turn right and you'll find yourself at the other set of level-crossing barriers.)

The path continues along Narrow Street past various modern blocks of flats, then past The Grapes, an ancient and much-loved riverside pub with a cosy interior and riverside terrace, dating back to 1583 and the model for the Six Jolly Fellowship Porters pub in Dickens' *Our Mutual Friend* (1864–5). Now owned by actor Sir Ian McKellen, it forms the end of a handsome row of 18th-century terraces, rather marooned amidst newer buildings. A little further on a signpost leads through gates back to the river, which starts to widen out here. The path continues past yet more flats and over a curved iron bridge. Passing under a girder that supports the balcony tower of the more imaginative apartment blocks, you soon reach Canary Riverside.

You're now walking along the west side of the Isle of Dogs. This area was left quite abandoned and desolate after the closing of the docks in the 1970s; its transformation into Canary Wharf, home to skyscrapers, investment banks and ever-increasing shopping and leisure facilities, is one of London's most extraordinary recent stories. A little further on, by Canary Wharf pier, is a parade of restaurants, while a flight of steps on your left leads to Canary Wharf station and shopping centre. Keep beside the river, past an impressive panoply of high-rise buildings to your left, then cross a dock to pass an odd stepped block of flats with circular balconies. Alongside the swish new flats a few remnants of the old Isle of Dogs remain, such as a tatty concrete pier, flanked by platforms that now function as observation posts for cormorants. This stretch of the river is not particularly scenic, but an excellent opportunity to compare the various architectural styles employed over the last couple of decades – note particularly the twin blocks each with a penthouse extending dizzyingly out into the space between them.

A little further on, an unexpected park opens up, a pleasant green space in the middle of the crush of buildings – this is Sir John McDougal Gardens, named after a local county councillor. There were once seven windmills here, built on a great bank of earth and stone – hence Millwall, the name of this area and the birthplace of the football club of the same name, now based across the river in Bermondsey. At the end of the park, follow the

the bollards by the river edge recall the ships once moored alongside. Out the other side the promenade passes a large apartment complex with blue balconies, then through the gates of the delightful Surrey Docks City Farm, which boasts an impressive herb and vegetable garden, a wide range of happily bleating animals humanely reared for meat and milk, and an excellent café open Wednesdays to Sundays. (When the gates to the farm are closed, turn right down to the road, along it and left back up Defoe Close.)

Beyond the farm are yet more flats, after which the path turns right under a web of rusting red girders and along a cobbled lane marked Commercial Pier Wharf, then left past Odessa Street Youth Club Sea Scouts' Hut.

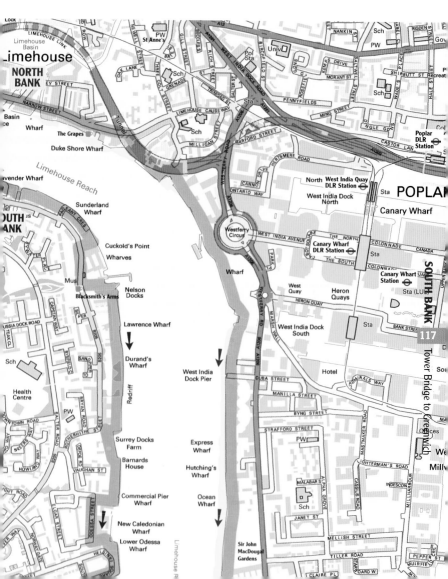

Tower Bridge to Greenwich

path alongside more flats – this time with balconies like spoked wheels – then go left inland.

At the T-junction ahead turn right past Arnhem Wharf Primary School on to Westferry Road, and through a scruffy urban landscape and past the Northern and Shell printing works, where the *Daily* and *Sunday Express* and *OK!* magazine are produced, amongst others. On your right an old dock, now a car park, offers a brief view of the river, but keep along the main road, passing a terrace of old dockers' cottages, then an extraordinary Victorian Romanesque basilica, now an arts and community centre. Claude Street, opposite it to your right, offers a tantalisingly short glimpse of the river.

You're finally allowed back on the riverbank via an alley leading right just after St Edward's School; cross the road

ahead and go into Ferguson Close and under a bland modern colonnade. Before you turn left along the river, pause to admire the remains of 18th-century Deptford on the opposite bank, now almost swallowed up by depressing modern dross. The path leads south past unexciting flats, with little to look at apart from occasional boats – and, across the river, the extraordinary six arches that are all that remains of a former warehouse. Passing Masthouse Terrace Pier, you'll notice an odd sort of park on your left: a sunken area of grass next to a warehouse, full not of trees and flowers but of long timbers lying parallel to each other on the ground. These are what remains of the launching site of the *Great Eastern*, built by Isambard Kingdom Brunel in 1857 and the largest ship in the world not only then but for the next 40 years. It was so enormous that it took Brunel

The Great Eastern under construction in 1857, dwarfing everything around it.

SOUTH BANK

Ship and Whale Wharf

Sir John
MacDougal
Gardens

NORTH BANK

Finland
Quay East

Rainbow
Quay

Greenland
Pier

Klein's
Wharf

Works

South Dock
(Marina)

St George's
Wharf

Millwall Outer Dock

Millwall

Isle of Dogs

St George's
Square

Pepys
Park

Liby

Britannia and
St Andrew's Wharves

Masthouse Terrace Pier

Burrell's Wharf

Palmer's
Wharf

Payne's
Wharf

When the road curves right towards the
Ship and Whale pub, keep straight on
down the alley ahead and left round
Odessa Wharf back to the river. Turn
right past flats; ahead is the old
Greenland Lock, which gives access to
South Dock. Make your way around it
and over the road bridge. Beyond is
Greenland Dock, laid out at the end of
the 17th century and London's oldest
riverside wet dock. Most of the
surrounding docks were filled in after
their closure in the 1970s, but this one
survived and became home to a
watersports centre.

Back on the river you pass Greenland
Pier, from which depart the Thames
Clippers to Greenwich and central
London, then cross over the working
lock which gives access to the marina.
You are now entering Deptford, which

has suffered perhaps the saddest decline
of any district of London. From the mid-
16th to late 19th centuries it was home
to the vast royal dockyard and for
centuries this was the administrative
hub of the Royal Navy. But as ships got
bigger and the river silted up, the
Deptford dockyard became less and less
practical, and it closed in 1869, since
when the area has gradually decayed, its
few architectural survivals lost amid ugly
post-war estates.

Keep along the riverside promenade,
past low-rise housing estates and a
tall green apartment block. Just
beyond it are a pair of fine dark-brick
buildings with arcades along the
lowest storey, remnants of the Navy
Victualling Yard that was based here
from 1788 to 1961. Turn right
between them, then across Bowditch

several attempts to launch the ship, rather embarrassingly as thousands of spectators came to watch the first try. A little further on is the site of what was once a factory producing chemical colours; its central building, the Plate House, is an odd fusion of warehouse and church styles, with an austere Romanesque turret.

Soon afterwards, past a row of incongruously Alpine-style terraces, the path starts to bend round to the left – and there suddenly the glorious splendour of neoclassical Greenwich appears before you, a vision from another world. Alas, all too soon the footpath ends in a car park just beyond the Elephant Royale restaurant and you must turn inland. Passing the cheerful Ferry House pub on your left, follow the signpost past Felstead Wharf down Ferry Street. When this unexciting road bends left, continue straight on; ahead on your right is Island Gardens park, right at the southern tip of the Isle of Dogs. Here ends the North Bank section of the Thames Path; from now on you have to follow the South Bank.

Turn left for Island Gardens DLR station; for Greenwich, turn right into the park and through the entrance of the sinister red-brick structure ahead, which takes you down a bleak, winding stairway, under the river and up and out again in Greenwich, where you can join the Thames Path on its southern side.

Tower Bridge to Greenwich

Greenwich from the southern tip of the Isle of Dogs: a sight it's hard to get tired of.

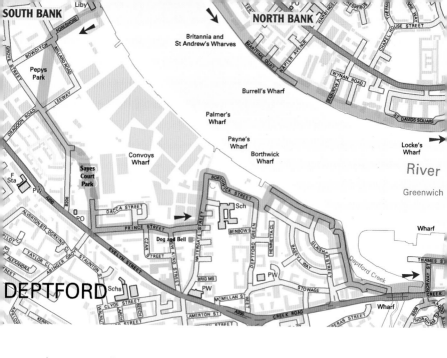

and past a vast, dirty-white block of flats. Follow the signpost left into Pepys Park and across it to the far left corner, then left along the road through a housing estate.

Just after you pass Hurlesh House on your right, turn left into Sayes Court Park, a peaceful space with a fine range of mature trees. The park is named after the house of the writer John Evelyn, who acquired it in 1653 and created one of England's most impressive gardens, with a long terrace, an orchard of hundreds of fruit trees and an ornamental lake with a summer house. Alas, in 1698 the youthful Peter the Great, Tsar of Russia, came to England to study shipbuilding and rented Evelyn's house for the duration. Peter and his entourage had no respect for property, using oil paintings as dartboards and wrecking the garden walls and hedges in their drunken

games. After some tense negotiations, the Treasury paid out £350 in compensation, but the house and garden were never the same again.

Follow the signpost right to skirt round a playground and exit the park via the gates to a cobbled street, then turn left at the top down Prince Street. Cross over the road junction with New King Street; as the road turns left soon afterwards a view opens up of the Canary Wharf towers, seemingly a world away. Just after the Dog and Bell pub (which boasts a charmingly old-fashioned pub sign and a decent offering of Belgian and other beers) turn left down Watergate Street. Sadly the water-gate is no longer accessible, but you can just see the roof of the building it belonged to: the old Master Shipwright's House, a beautiful Queen Anne mansion built in 1708 at the peak of Deptford's glory.

The entrance to the Surrey Docks, c.1930; note the amazing variety of boats at work.

The Port of London

London has been a port for as long as it has been a city; its first harbour was built by the Romans, and before long goods were being traded regularly from all over Europe. For many centuries trading vessels docked and unloaded their cargoes in the Pool of London, downriver from London Bridge, where the Customs House still stands today. However, by the late 18th century overcrowding had become so acute that ships had to wait months to unload. Something had to be done; and in 1799 the West India Dock Company Act was passed, allowing the transformation of virtually the entire Isle of Dogs into a vast series of enclosed docks.

Three more dock complexes swiftly followed – the London Docks in Wapping, the Surrey Dock across the river in Rotherhithe, and the East India Dock downriver at Blackwall. Between them they transformed some 300 acres of marshy land into artificial basins and, with the associated wharfs, warehouses and approach roads, changed the eastern half of London for ever. There was no shortage of ships to fill up the docks; as Britain's empire expanded, London became the epicentre of global trade. Goods of every possible type, from every possible source, came up the Thames, as many evocative street and place names bear witness:

Cinnamon Wharf, Greenland Dock, Tobacco Dock, Paper Mill Wharf, Gallions Reach.

As ships got bigger and the river silted up, docks were built deeper and further downriver, with the enormous Royal Docks extending far east of the Isle of Dogs. In 1908 the docks were nationalised to become part of the new Port of London Authority, which ever since has been responsible for the tidal Thames from Teddington to the sea. By the 1930s the London docklands took up 26 square miles, stretching 10 miles east of Tower Bridge on both sides of the river, and the port and docks combined employed some 100,000 men.

The years 1962–4 saw record tonnages handled in the Port of London. Its lasting future seemed assured. But in fact quite the opposite happened – within 20 years every one of the London docks had closed. The swift rise of container shipping, which required vessels too enormous to squeeze up the Thames and into the ageing docks, coupled with neverending industrial disputes, dealt a crushing blow, and in October 1981 the last ship sailed out of the last dock to remain open. Today the old West India Docks site is home to the financial district of Canary Wharf – which makes its money from virtual rather than physical transactions, but is just as central to global commerce as was its watery predecessor.

Turn right down Borthwick Street, with the incongruously named Twinkle Park on your right, and on your left a battered brick warehouse façade – a melancholy sight that exemplifies Deptford's history. Follow Watergate Street round to the left. When the road turns right keep ahead, following the Thames Path signpost around a boatyard and, finally, back to the river.

Follow the path towards Greenwich, then inland down Deptford Creek, a muddy tidal waterway that carries the River Ravensbourne into the Thames. On your left you can see the domed tower of St Alphege's Church, built by Nicholas Hawksmoor, and to its right the roof of the Royal Observatory with its red time ball, which since 1833 has dropped at 1 p.m. every day to enable watchers to synchronise their clocks to Greenwich Mean Time. Look out for the statue of Peter the Great, a gift from Russia to mark the tercentenary of the Tsar's time in London.

The path enters a housing estate, then leads to the noisy main road. Turn left and over the bridge across the creek, then left down Norway Street, which bends right at the old Thames pub.

Turn left down Horseferry Place, then right along the river. A couple of old cannons recall the area's more warlike days – then look up ahead of you and you'll see the *Cutty Sark*, a many-masted tea clipper built in 1869 and badly damaged in a fire in 2007, but now restored to her former glory.

To your left is the entrance to the Greenwich foot tunnel, which takes you under the Thames to Island Gardens on the north bank; turn right for Greenwich centre and Cutty Sark DLR station.

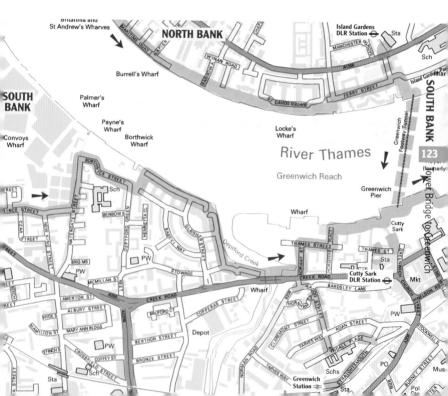

A Canal Diversion

Circular walk from Limehouse
6 miles (9.6 km)

If the Thames is London's highway, the canals are its back streets – for many years grimy and industrial, then neglected and litter-ridden, but now (mostly) clean, attractive and much loved by walkers, boaters and cyclists. This pleasantly varied walk through revitalised East London offers a refreshing contrast to the river, and gives you the opportunity to inspect four different stretches of canal, London's oldest public park and the 2012 Olympic site.

From the Narrow Street road bridge, take the path down into the marina, cross left over the lock and continue clockwise around Limehouse Basin. (If you're starting from Limehouse station, turn down Branch Road and then left into the marina after Berglen Court.) Follow the marina round towards the railway bridge, then right alongside it until you reach the lock that marks the entrance to the Regent's Canal (named after the Prince Regent, later George IV, during whose rule the canal was started in 1812).

Cross over the curvy pedestrian bridge, then turn left under the road and railway bridges on to the canal towpath. The difference in scale and atmosphere from the river path is immediately noticeable – low bridges pass overhead at regular intervals and in place of imposing riverside buildings you're hemmed in on both sides by a scruffy but not unattractive combination of blocks of flats and untended greenery.

The path rises towards Salmon Lane Lock, then passes under overhanging trees and a railway bridge. Just beyond it rises a heavily graffitied brick chimney, still in use as a sewer ventilation shaft. An area of grassland to your right has been planted with wildflowers to soften this slightly bleak corner – one of many examples of

the efforts made to improve London's environment in recent years. Just beyond the next bridge is the Ragged School Museum, once home to Dr Barnardo's first 'ragged school' for poor local children. The museum includes a recreation of a Victorian classroom and kitchen, and is open every Wednesday and Thursday and the first Sunday afternoon of each month.

The path rises again to Johnson's Lock; soon afterwards it joins Mile End Park, which follows the canal all the way north to the junction with the Hertford Union Canal. The land that now makes up the park was devastated by a Second World War bombing raid, and lay neglected until a concerted effort was made to develop it just before the millennium – very successfully so, as the hordes of locals strolling, running or cycling through it bear testimony. A few hundred yards on is the Mile End Road bridge; *for Mile End tube station take the steps up on the other side.* On the wall to your right is mounted, rather incongruously, a pub sign for the New Globe on Mile End Road. In the mid-19th century the land alongside the canal was part of the New Globe Tavern gardens, which offered music, firework displays and hot-air balloon rides to an appreciative clientele.

Continue past Mile End Lock (look out for the peculiar modern extension to the lock-keeper's cottage) and into a beautifully landscaped parkland area, with man-made wildlife ponds and an ecology pavilion off to the right. There are always several narrowboats moored along this stretch, most painted in cheerful colours and immaculately kept. Trains clatter across the wide railway bridge ahead – this is the main line out to Essex; a little further on is a reedbed habitat, surrounding a small waterlily-bedecked lake.

Soon after passing under Roman Road bridge, you'll see the towpath ascend sharply to a cobbled bridge. This is the junction with the Hertford Union Canal,

opened in 1830 as a shortcut between the Regent's Canal and the River Lea, which you'll now follow. At the top of the rise, turn right off the towpath, round and down again to join the Hertford Union. A typically mixed East End landscape follows – old industrial buildings, new flats, converted warehouses, houseboats in every possible state of repair. Appearances can be deceptive – the red-brick warehouse on the right soon after the Grove Roadbridge looks derelict at first sight, but is actually home to the thriving Chisenhale Gallery.

After the Slew Bridge on Old Ford Road, the canal runs alongside Victoria Park, which was opened in 1845 in response to concerns that the local population had no green spaces for exercise and recreation. It has been much loved and used ever since, and amongst other amenities houses a boating lake, a café and – most excitingly for the Thames enthusiast – two pedestrian alcoves from Old London Bridge, located at the east end of the park by the path that runs north up to Hackney Wick.

The park disappears from view by Hertford Union Top Lock, with its charming lock-keeper's cottage. Keeping along the towpath, you'll soon encounter the Middle and Bottom Locks – between them a bridge carrying the fearsome A12 – as the canal descends toward the River Lee Navigation. This is a stretch of canal cut through in 1768 to provide a navigable waterway for boats travelling between Hertfordshire and the Thames; the River Lea (or Lee) itself takes a complicated winding route that is hard for larger vessels to negotiate.

Right ahead, on the far side of the T-junction at which the Hertford Union Canal meets the Lee Navigation, is the 2012 Olympics site. On your right is the imposing yet graceful stadium, Anish Kapoor's twisted metal sculpture behind it, and to its left Zaha Hadid's swimming pool with its wave-like roof. Turn left along the Lee Navigation then over the bridge ahead, and back towards the stadium with Canary Wharf beyond.

Just past the stadium is Old Ford Lock, at which point the waterway is joined by the old River Lea, which you cross via a narrow bridge. Continue in the same direction; after passing under the road bridge, turn back to admire the Metropolitan Board of Works black plaque identifying the Northern Outfall Sewer, built in 1862–3 as part of Joseph Bazalgette's great sewerage masterplan (see page 86).

The towpath continues through a mix of greenery and post-industrial grubbiness. Just behind the London Concrete works you'll see an incongruous brick tower – this is part of the old Bryant and May match factory, famous for the strike of 1888, when match-girls successfully stood up against appalling working conditions. You'll get a better view of it when you've gone past the bridge, after which you encounter a veritable transport maelstrom – a major railway bridge, then on your right the vast road junction where the A12 meets the A11/A118. It's all offensively noisy, but keep your nerve and cross the elaborate wooden-railinged bridge, then under the concrete bridge, and the tumult gradually starts to subside into comparative peace.

As the river curves round to the right, the cobbled towpath leads up to a pair of bridges. Cross the second one, and you'll be confronted with one of London's most unexpected sights: a delightful array of 18th- and 19th-century warehouses and a cobbled courtyard, seemingly untouched by modern times, and with two charming watermills rising gracefully over the scene. This is Three Mills Island, whose history can be traced back to the 12th century. A film and television studio is now based here, and the larger mill – the House Mill – is owned by a local trust and open to visitors on summer Sunday afternoons. *To reach Bromley by Bow underground* station, turn right over the bridge towards Tesco, then left towards the main road and under the underpass.

Turn right down the river – parallel to it on your left is the Three Mills Wall River – and under the railway bridge. Ahead loom the towers of Canary Wharf. Before you now are Bow Locks, through which boats can travel down Bow Creek and into the Thames at Blackwall. Having crossed the locks – on rather a pretty moulded concrete bridge – continue straight ahead, then take the walkway along the water, now the Limehouse Cut, and under another vast road bridge, this time the A12 Blackwall Tunnel Approach, and the towpath continues past various warehouses and old industrial sites, then under a blue railway bridge and grey road bridge, and alongside more modern flats.

Continue for 1 mile (1.6 km) along this quiet stretch, the only noise the squeaking of coots and the distant hum of traffic, circumnavigating Abbotts Wharf Moorings. Bow Common, Burdett Road and Commercial Road bridges roar overhead, then a bridge carrying the Docklands Light Railway, beautifully designed in contrasting brickwork. A little further on the canal veers right – look back to admire the turreted tower of Hawksmoor's St Anne's Limehouse – and into Limehouse Marina. Turn left round the basin until you reach the great lock that forms the entrance to the Thames. Here you can ascend to Narrow Street and turn either left to rejoin the Thames Path, or right over the road bridge, right again through the fountained plaza and then straight ahead up Branch Road to find Limehouse station.

Three Mills Island, an enchanting remnant of old London.

7 Greenwich to Woolwich

including Thames Path Extension from Thames Barrier to Woolwich

5¾ miles/9.25 km
(Greenwich to North Greenwich 2½ miles/4 km,
North Greenwich to Woolwich 3¼ miles/5.2 km)

WARNING: much of this stretch is being redeveloped, so watch out for diversions and alterations.

From Cutty Sark DLR station, turn left through the arcade, then left again past the Cutty Sark. At the entrance to the Greenwich Foot Tunnel, turn right on to the Thames Path.

Turn right along the river, passing Greenwich Pier, from which boats run by Thames Clipper, City Cruises and Thames River Services depart. As the promenade turns right you'll see before you an unparalleled view of the magnificent Royal Naval College. In front of it is a pink obelisk dedicated to Joseph Bellot, who died in 1853 on an expedition in search of the lost explorer Sir John Franklin.

Follow the narrow path that runs in front of the Royal Naval College; you may hear the strains of students practising at the nearby Trinity College of Music, now based

here. Gorgeous wrought-iron gates on your right lead through the complex and to the National Maritime Museum beyond.

The path turns inland and left round the ever-popular Trafalgar Tavern, then down a paved alley past another pub, The Yacht, and a row of Victorian terraced cottages. The alley leads into a lovely riverside garden in front of the Trinity Hospital almshouse, founded in 1616, rebuilt in the current crenellated style in 1812, and still fulfilling its original role as sheltered housing for the elderly. Look for the plaque on the river wall marking the high-water mark of the 1928 Thames flood, which killed 14 people in Pimlico and was a contributing factor in the construction of the Thames Barrier.

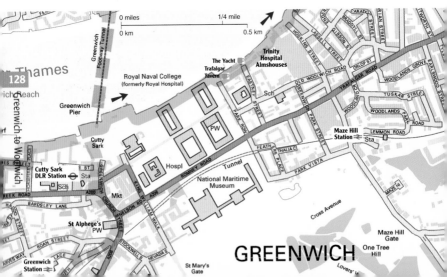

The Royal Naval College from the Thames Path, with the Queen's House just visible in the distance.

Maritime Greenwich

Greenwich is one of the great joys of the London Thames. It first entered the history books thanks to Greenwich Palace, where King Henry VIII and Queen Elizabeth I were born in 1491 and 1533 respectively. The palace later fell into disrepair, and in 1664 Charles II decided to pull it down and build a new palace for himself on the same site. The architect John Webb made a start on the right-hand block (as seen from the river), but Charles lost interest and nothing more happened until, in 1694, Christopher Wren was commissioned to finish the complex as a Royal Hospital for Seamen, akin to the Royal Hospital Chelsea (page 74) he had built in the previous decade.

Wren and his successor architects (who included the equally talented Nicholas Hawksmoor, also the designer of nearby St Alphege's Church) succeeded in creating one of London's most beautiful sets of buildings. Now known as the Royal Naval College, which function it fulfilled from 1873 to 1998, from the Thames it presents a fantastic Baroque panorama,

its elaborate classical colonnades lifted by the twin domes with their gleaming pinnacles. The domes mark the presence of the Chapel and Painted Hall respectively; both are as gorgeous inside as out, and open daily at no charge.

Between and behind the two halves of the Royal Naval College can be seen the Queen's House, a square villa designed by Inigo Jones for Queen Anne of Denmark, James I's wife, in 1616. Britain's first example of classical architecture, it is a simple and lovely building that is now part of the National Maritime Museum, itself one of London's major tourist attractions. The museum deserves a dedicated visit, including as it does the Royal Observatory, location of the Prime Meridian (hence Greenwich Mean Time) and a rolling series of excellent special exhibitions. Entrance to the permanent collection is free, and amongst its many joys (including a fantastic Maritime London gallery) is the chance to see the magnificent gilded barge built for Frederick, Prince of Wales, in 1732 and used for many stately progresses along the Thames, often with an accompanying musicians' boat.

Just beyond the almshouse is the grim but rather majestic Greenwich Power Station, which, despite its rather dilapidated appearance is also still fulfilling its original role, though it is now powered by gas rather than the original coal. Continue along the river, under the jetty once used to unload coal and take away the resulting ash, and past a handsome row of Georgian terraces which houses the Cutty Sark pub, more peaceful than its central Greenwich competitors. At the end of the terraces is the freestanding Harbour Master's Office on Ballast Quay, which dates to 1855.

Keep ahead up the ramp beyond, then right in front of some particularly shiny new flats, down the steps on the other side and left down the lane through the rest of the new housing estate. After the first block of flats on your right, look out for a narrow path leading off to your left, with hoardings on either side. Follow this path (which was marked as temporary at the time of writing, and therefore may move) and turn right at the end, where you'll find yourself back by the river, with a view of the Canary Wharf towers.

This stretch of the path is isolated – there is no way on or off it for almost a mile – but enjoyable, with working vessels on the river and industrial structures from Victorian times to the present day on your right. Eventually the path turns right, with the gasworks visible ahead. Turn left down another narrow fenced path and you'll see the yellow spars of the O2 Arena to your right, with Greenwich Power Station across the water. The path becomes broader and soon returns to the river proper, passing the Victoria Deep Water Terminal, where large ships can often be seen being loaded with aggregate. This is a working site, so keep a look out for heavy vehicles.

Before long the path veers briefly inland around a small inlet, then curves round to circumnavigate the vast O2 Arena. Built in 1999 as the much-mocked Millennium Dome, this extraordinary edifice – now a major London landmark with its pale roof membrane suspended from narrow yellow spars – has become one of Europe's most successful music venues. Look out for Ordnance Jetty on your left,

The O2 Arena, once a derided white elephant, now a much-loved music venue.

View over the Thames from the east side of the North Greenwich Peninsula, a characteristic mix of greenery, new buildings and old industry.

a disused pier now being transformed into a wildlife habitat. Just beyond it is a vertical section, including the bridge, of an old sand dredger; now titled *Slice of Reality*, it was created by Richard Wilson as part of the Millennium Dome project.

This area is Blackwall Point; in the 17th century the bodies of executed pirates were displayed here in cages as a warning to their would-be imitators. The marshy land later became devoted to industry, with a huge gasworks and a power station taking up hundreds of acres of land. Both closed in the late 20th century, leaving vast areas derelict; since 1997 much redevelopment has taken place (and is still ongoing). Fortunately, attitudes towards the natural environment have become increasingly enlightened during this period; a display board describes how the river bank here has been

carefully designed to encourage birds, salt-water plants and invertebrates.

As you leave the view of Canary Wharf behind you, planes descending over your head to nearby City Airport, look across to the opposite bank for an old-fashioned lighthouse, almost lost in the midst of newer buildings. This is Trinity Buoy Wharf, built in 1864–6 for lighting experiments and training lighthouse keepers, and now a characterful centre for the arts. Beyond it the northern shore is still predominantly industrial rather than residential, though various hopeful blocks of flats poke their heads above the chemical plants and heaps of gravel.

The riverside promenade continues, passing towering glassy blocks of flats on the right. Ahead is North Greenwich Pier; if you need a break, turn inland here to the Peninsula shopping plaza for cafés and restaurants, or for North Greenwich underground station. A little further on you'll see a flock of small yachts, their fixings clinking in the wind, forming a pleasant contrast to the new Greenwich Millennium Village developments. A few hundred yards on is the charming Greenwich Peninsula Ecology Park, which boasts closely planted alders and a pretty boardwalk overlooking a man-made lake. Just beyond it, the path veers briefly inland round Greenwich Yacht Club, then back to the river and under an array of rusted iron girders, part of an industrial site through which the path now leads.

Continue straight on round an inlet and past industrial buildings; a little further on you'll pass the home of the London Port Health Authority, which checks imported foodstuffs and watches out for infectious diseases. This stretch of the path is not exactly scenic but nevertheless has its charms, offering as it does an insight into what is still a working river. Just after the Anchor and Hope pub, a local favourite, a road leads off to the right to Charlton station, ½ mile (0.8 km) away.

Keep straight on, and almost immediately you'll see the Thames Barrier, with its nine steel piers like upturned boat keels. As you get closer you'll see that each includes a smaller 'keel' behind, with what looks like a yellow crane in the middle. This is the operating machinery for the gates that form the Barrier, which spend most of the time resting on concrete sills in the riverbed. When a tidal surge is forecast they are raised to form a continuous wall across the river, controlling the volume of water that can rush up the estuary and hence preventing flooding upriver. The Thames Barrier started operating in 1982 and has been raised more than 110 times so far, playing a vital role in keeping London safe.

Woolwich Dockyard, as depicted by Nicholas Pocock in 1790.

Woolwich Royal Dockyard

Founded by King Henry VIII in 1512, Woolwich (along with Deptford) played a crucial role in the development of the Royal Navy. Henry's flagship the *Henry Grace à Dieu* was built here in 1514, and as the dockyard expanded a large network of naval craftsmen soon grew up around it – ropemakers, sawyers, sailmakers and coopers, not to mention forgotten trades such as caulkers, hewers and clinchers, all working under the direction of the Master Shipwright.

Many other famous ships were built here, including HMS *Beagle*, launched in 1820, in which Charles Darwin made his first ground-breaking scientific voyages. Alas, as warships grew larger and the Thames silted up, Deptford and Woolwich became increasingly outdated compared to the Chatham Royal Dockyard further down the coast. Both closed in 1869, and only tantalising fragments remain.

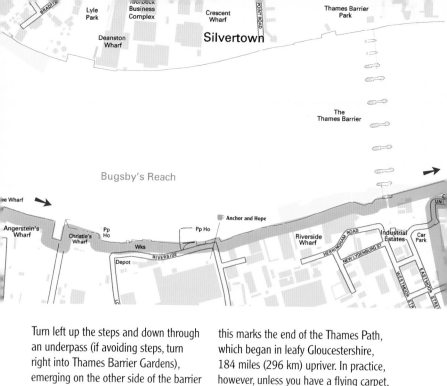

Lyle Park

Deanston Wharf

Business Complex

Crescent Wharf

POINT ROAD

Silvertown

Thames Barrier Park

The Thames Barrier

Bugsby's Reach

e Wharf

Angerstein's Wharf

Christie's Wharf

Pp Ho

Wks

Depot

RIVERSIDE

Pp Ho

Anchor and Hope

Riverside Wharf

HERRINGHAM ROAD

NEW LYDENBURG ST

Industrial Estates

Car Park

UNI

Turn left up the steps and down through an underpass (if avoiding steps, turn right into Thames Barrier Gardens), emerging on the other side of the barrier to reach a terraced grassy bank with a playground and a basic but welcome café, which is also home to the Thames Barrier Information Centre. Technically this marks the end of the Thames Path, which began in leafy Gloucestershire, 184 miles (296 km) upriver. In practice, however, unless you have a flying carpet, you'll probably want to continue along the Thames Path Extension for another mile (1.6 km) to Woolwich for public transport options.

The Thames Barrier, without which London would be at risk of disastrous flooding.

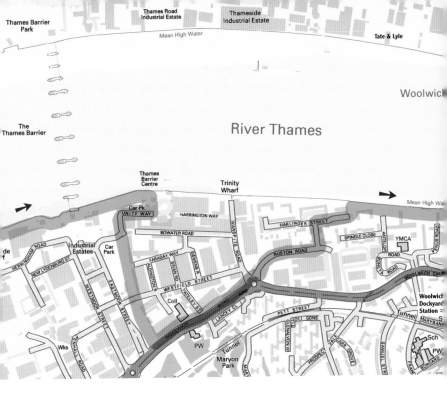

The stretch of river path east of the Thames Barrier will be opened to the public at some point, but at the time of writing the Thames Path Extension runs inland for its first ½ mile (0.8 km). Take the steps down by the café and then double back along the lane until you reach Thames Barrier Gardens. Follow the signpost inland, with the Barrier behind you, walking between flowerbeds and past a wildflower mound until you reach the now-closed Thames Barrier Arms pub at the rear of the park.

Cross the road and continue through a small tree-filled park, coming out on the noisy Woolwich Road. Turn left along the road, then at a roundabout turn half-left down Ruston Road. On your right you'll see a towering brick chimney, which was built in 1837 for a steam factory in the Royal Dockyard here.

Just after you pass some old dock buildings on your right, turn left into a low-rise estate and then right down Harlinger Street. You'll soon see the vast Tate & Lyle works across the Thames; at the end of the road turn left through the gates to rejoin the riverside promenade. Turn right then up the steps to a prow-shaped viewpoint, and down the other side (a ramp provides step-free access) and past two gun emplacements, which signal the nearby presence of Woolwich Arsenal.

Ahead you'll see two vast gateways, one on either side of the river, and running between them the Woolwich Ferry, the only way by which vehicles can travel between the north and south banks of the Thames until the Dartford Tunnel further into the estuary. The path passes

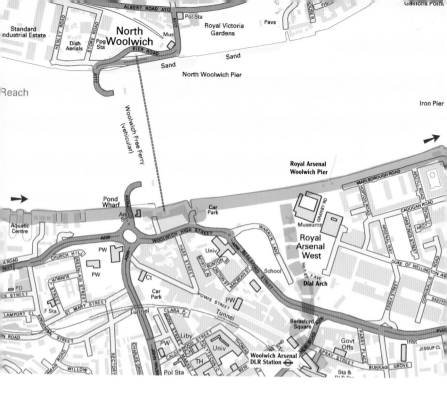

a run of disused docks, now leafy and overgrown. Cross over the approach road to the ferry and then take the road down on the other side past the London Ambulance Service hut. At the junction ahead, turn left (even if you want to get to Woolwich Arsenal station, which is confusingly signposted right). Follow the riverside promenade past the Waterfront Leisure Centre, round a small inlet and out into a grassy plaza with a skateboarding rink in the middle. Beyond is the impressive Woolwich Arsenal site (see page 141), with Woolwich Pier on your left.

Turn right through the Woolwich Arsenal site and out through the gate on the other side. Cross the road and keep straight on through Beresford Square. Woolwich Arsenal DLR and railway station is on your left.

The imposing gatehouse of Woolwich Arsenal adds a touch of class to the busy local market.

THAMES PATH EXTENSION

Woolwich To Crayford Ness

Maritime Greenwich and the Isle of Dogs:
a fine mix of old and new.

8½ miles/13.7 km
(Woolwich to Erith 7 miles/ 11.2 km, Erith to Crayford Ness 1½ miles/ 2.4 km)
plus 1½ miles/ 2.4 km from Crayford Ness to Slade Green station

From Woolwich Arsenal station, take the exit marked 'Town Centre', coming out in Beresford Square. On your right you will see the grand Royal Arsenal gatehouse – turn towards this through the square, then cross Beresford Street at the traffic lights just behind the gatehouse. Go through the gates into the Royal Arsenal site and continue straight on to the river.

Ahead, flanked by two octagonal gatehouses, is the Royal Arsenal Woolwich Pier, served by Thames Clipper services to central London in the mornings and evenings. Here you join the Thames Path Extension, turning right towards a cluster of white blocks of flats. On your right is a fine array of original Arsenal buildings, all designed with an attention to detail and proportion that is hard to imagine in their modern equivalents.

At the boundary of the Royal Arsenal site, the path curves right inland around an old dock; take the steps up and round a blue viewing platform, or keep on the paved path for step-free access. The path here is broad and well designed, with plenty of room for walkers, runners and cyclists. On your left note the broad expanse of the Thames foreshore at low tide – a particularly rich ecosystem here, as the numbers of gulls and other birds make clear.

A few hundred yards further on, pass through some battered blue gates and on to a gravel path between trees, along which it continues past new flats and sprawling greenery, quiet but for the planes taking off from City Airport across the river. After about ½ mile (0.8 km) a

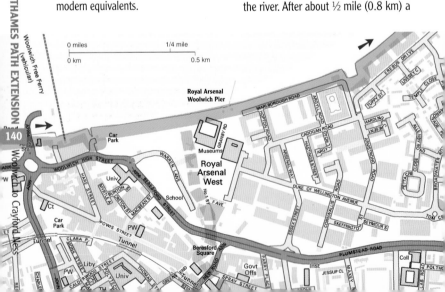

The Old Royal Military Academy, Woolwich, built in 1720.

Royal Arsenal, Woolwich

An arms storage depot was first established here in 1671, to be joined in due course by an ammunition laboratory and a gun foundry. The complex grew and developed over the centuries, playing a crucial role in the research and manufacture of armaments and explosives in the Peninsula and Crimean Wars; at its peak, during the First World War, the Royal Arsenal extended over 1,300 acres and employed about 80,000 people. During the Second World War the Arsenal suffered many bombing raids, and the site declined gradually over the following decades, with the ordnance factories closing in 1967 and the Ministry of Defence finally taking its leave in 1994.

Much of the enormous Arsenal site has inevitably been sold off as building land, but the splendid historic centre remains, and to its great fortune it has been redeveloped sympathetically and with an eye to its heritage. The complex is very rewarding to explore, with well-designed information boards that identify the various structures and explain the historical context.

Particularly notable is the Royal Brass Foundry, on the left as you enter. Built in 1717, it's attributed to the great Baroque architect Sir John Vanbrugh; its magnificent doorway, with its stone and brick striped piers and royal arms above, is testimony to the significance of the Arsenal's national role. From the same period is the Old Royal Military Academy, which boasts another fine entrance, guarded by a lion and a unicorn.

On its right, part of the old Royal Laboratory, is the Greenwich Heritage Centre (open Tuesday to Saturday), an excellent free museum that tells the history of the Woolwich Dockyard and Arsenal. Opposite you'll see Firepower!, the Royal Artillery Museum, housed in the old Paper Cartridge Factory. Open between Wednesday and Sunday, it's intelligently laid out to appeal both to those interested in British military history and to children more excited by bangs, flashes and the re-creation of artillery bombardments.

The Royal Arsenal left one final legacy, which is to be seen not in Woolwich but on television screens all over the world: Arsenal football team, 'The Gunners', established here in 1886, which moved to north London in 1913.

Woolwich to Crayford Ness

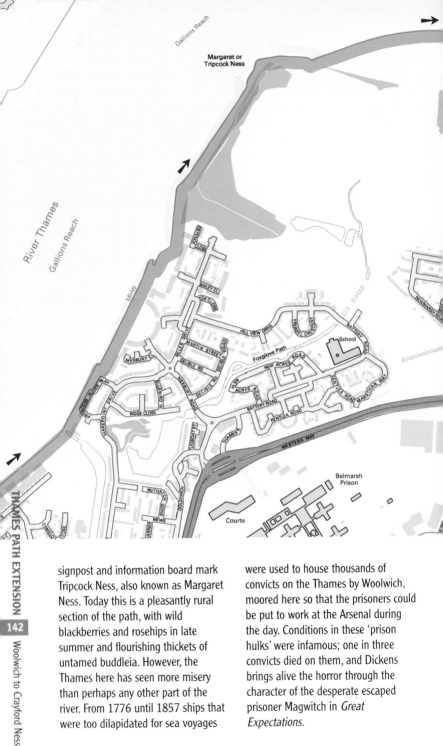

signpost and information board mark Tripcock Ness, also known as Margaret Ness. Today this is a pleasantly rural section of the path, with wild blackberries and rosehips in late summer and flourishing thickets of untamed buddleia. However, the Thames here has seen more misery than perhaps any other part of the river. From 1776 until 1857 ships that were too dilapidated for sea voyages were used to house thousands of convicts on the Thames by Woolwich, moored here so that the prisoners could be put to work at the Arsenal during the day. Conditions in these 'prison hulks' were infamous; one in three convicts died on them, and Dickens brings alive the horror through the character of the desperate escaped prisoner Magwitch in *Great Expectations*.

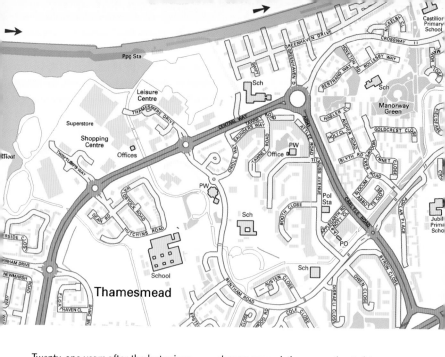

Thamesmead

Twenty-one years after the last prison hulk burnt down, this same stretch of river saw Britain's worst-ever peacetime disaster. In September 1878 a paddle steamer, the *Princess Alice*, was making her way back up the Thames after a day trip to Sheerness, further out into the estuary. Crammed with perhaps 900 happy holidaymakers, she was rounding Tripcock Ness when a vast coal steamer, the *Bywell Castle*, loomed into view from the other side of the point. Overcome by panic, the captain of the *Princess Alice* turned the wrong way and the *Bywall Castle* slammed into her, sinking the pleasure steamer within minutes. Hundreds of men, women and children were left struggling in the water, which itself was foully polluted with industrial waste from the factories on both shores and sewage from Crossness and Barking pumping stations nearby. They had little chance of survival. Over the next few days more than 650 bodies were recovered, and

dozens more victims are estimated to have been swept out to sea, or to have died later from the effects of swallowing poisoned water.

Shortly afterwards, the path forks into a pedestrian route to the left and a cycleway to the right. Taking the former, continue along the river. On the other side of the water you'll see what looks like a vast concrete portcullis – this is the Barking Barrier, which guards the entrance to the River Roding, and can be lowered to prevent flooding at high tide. After a few hundred yards the path comes out in a small tree-filled plaza; a little further on a concrete ramp leads up to a windowless box that is Lake Four Pumping Station.

Keep on the pedestrian path by the river, which soon runs in front of a gabled housing development. This is the edge of Thamesmead, built on part of the old Arsenal site from the late 1960s onwards. At a time when the

Map labels: Cross Ness; ST ANDREWS CLOSE; Mean High Water; Halfway Reach; REDBOURNE DRIVE; SALTWAY DRIVE; ENDURE CLOSE; GALE; CH; Golf Driving; Outfalls; CHERBURY CLOSE; Crossness Pumping Station; Golf Course; LONGWORTH; COURTLAND; KINGFISHER CL; HALSHAM CLOSE; FLEMING WAY; BAYLISS AVENUE; CROSSWAY; LEDLOW; KINDER CL; HALD; DEN WAY; HOWD; THAMESMEET W; HAMESBANK PL; ROAD; CRESS; PARKER CLOSE; MANOR CROSS; CROSSWAY; EASTGATE CL; TEMPLAR DRIVE; CUMBERTON WAY; ANTHONY CLOSE

failings of previous inner-city housing estates were already becoming clear, Thamesmead was seen as representing a new style of urban design, 'a town for the 21st century', centred around the lakes and waterways that provided drainage for the underlying marshlands. However, as so often in the saga of post-war planning, the vision failed to be reflected in the reality. The innovative high-level walkways between blocks became heavily littered and unsafe, and the waterways and generous provision of green space

resulted in a sprawling settlement that feels strangely isolated, not helped by limited public transport and a serious lack of shops and other local amenities.

Continue along the river for ½ mile (0.8 km) or so, past deep flowerbeds and locals fishing in the river. After three turquoise shelters shaped like upturned keels, the promenade becomes a gravel path, curving gradually right with a view of wind turbines ahead on the opposite bank. Before long you will see before you a large white building, with a curved roof and a broad green stripe curling around it; nestling in front of it is a square brick edifice, much older, and trimmed in red and white. As a faint tang in the air suggests, you have arrived at a sacred place for waste-management devotees: Crossness.

In fact, easy though it is to be flippant, this is a fascinating site for anyone interested in how a modern city works. Crossness Pumping Station played a

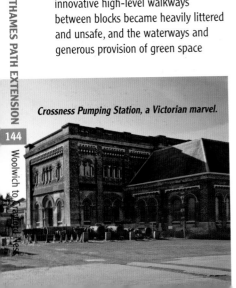

Crossness Pumping Station, a Victorian marvel.

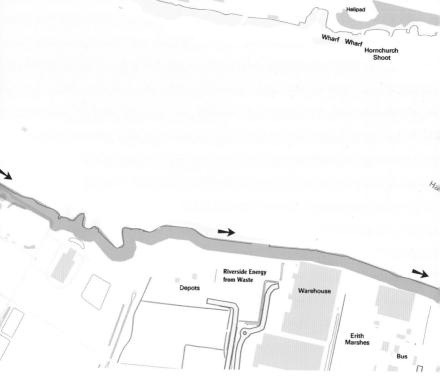

crucial role in the visionary drainage system masterminded by Sir Joseph Bazalgette in the 1860s (see page 86). It was here that the great Southern Outfall Sewer, carrying sewage piped from across south London, emptied into a vast storage reservoir and was released into the Thames at high tide, to be carried away into the North Sea.

Like its fellow pumping stations at Abbey Mills and Chelsea, Crossness was an architectural as well as an industrial marvel. Designed in a style known as Rundbogenstil ('round arched style'), essentially an industrial Romanesque, its façade reflects an attention to colour and detail that is matched by that of the glorious polychromatic interior. After the pumping station was closed in 1953, it was abandoned to decay and

vandalism for many years. However, thanks to a determined band of steam enthusiasts, in 1987 the Crossness Engines Trust was set up, with a remit to restore and preserve the pumping station to its original glory. One of the four great pumping engines, Prince Consort, is now working again, and a new access road and visitor centre is nearing completion.

The Thames Path runs round Crossness on the river side, offering an excellent view of the exterior. Information boards explain the history of the site, and screens with viewholes offer an opportunity to admire the many birds that feast on the shoreline at low tide – including redshank, lapwings and a host of waterfowl rarely seen within London's perimeter. Note the jetty, once used for the sludge boats that from 1887 until 1998 made daily journeys to carry solid sewage out into the North Sea. It's now used by 'bubblers', Thames Water boats that pump oxygen into the river when it's needed to sustain water life.

Follow the path along the river (look out for the charming if unconvincing reconstructions of Thames life in previous ages). Next on your right is a modern sewage plant, one of Europe's largest, with vast concrete beds surrounded by crowds of hopeful starlings. Keep along the undulating path (depending on which way the wind is blowing, you may want to walk quite swiftly at this point) and soon you'll emerge into fresher air beside the gleaming sludge-powered generator, built in 1998, which burns treated sewage to produce energy, replacing the sludge boats.

Continue along the tarmac path – on either side you can see the marshes that would once have covered this

entire region – and pass through a gate. Just ahead of you is a vast white building bearing a green stripe: this is the Riverside Energy from Waste facility, the latest addition to the Crossness complex. Non-recyclable rubbish is brought here from several London boroughs – most of it carried down the Thames on barges – and incinerated, generating electricity which is fed back into the National Grid.

If you feel the need of a break from waste management, look across the river: there you'll see the Ford Dagenham car factory, which has been in operation since 1931, employing as many as 40,000 people in the post-war years. It was originally established on the Thames to receive waterborne deliveries of coal and steel; these days it has a much smaller workforce and builds vehicle engines rather than whole cars, but it's still an important industrial location and its diesel-engine

The grand opening of Crossness Pumping Station in 1865; the interior is now being restored to its former glory.

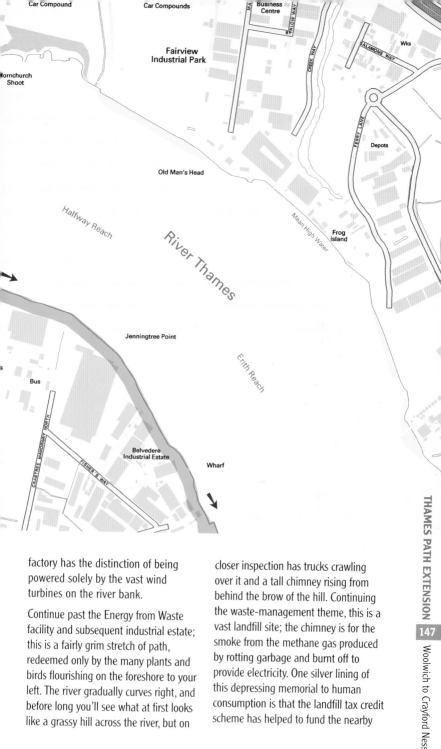

factory has the distinction of being powered solely by the vast wind turbines on the river bank.

Continue past the Energy from Waste facility and subsequent industrial estate; this is a fairly grim stretch of path, redeemed only by the many plants and birds flourishing on the foreshore to your left. The river gradually curves right, and before long you'll see what at first looks like a grassy hill across the river, but on

closer inspection has trucks crawling over it and a tall chimney rising from behind the brow of the hill. Continuing the waste-management theme, this is a vast landfill site; the chimney is for the smoke from the methane gas produced by rotting garbage and burnt off to provide electricity. One silver lining of this depressing memorial to human consumption is that the landfill tax credit scheme has helped to fund the nearby

Erith Marshes, an uncanny and oddly beautiful landscape.

Following another couple of piers on your left the path becomes greener again, and less remote; blocks of flats start to appear on your right, and the path winds past jetties and walls with fearsome spikes on top. After a few hundred yards it snakes inland around an old dock.

If you want to call a halt to your day's walking here, take the paved path at the inside corner of the dock up to the main road, cross the high street and take the first right down Stonewood Road to Erith railway station.

If you're continuing to the bitter end, follow the dock the whole way round and turn right at the river along the paved promenade in front of Erith Riverside Gardens, a pretty park filled with plants specially chosen for the windy and salty conditions. At Erith Causeway, the path turns right up a ramp to the main road. (If you feel the need for refreshment, the Running Horses pub to your right is always popular; alternatively, try the Potion bar further up the hill, or Mambocino Coffee in the Riverside shopping centre beyond.)

Rainham Marshes bird reserve, and from 2018 the entire landfill site is planned to be transformed into a nature reserve.

Passing a battered jetty to your left and the yellow and black gates of an industrial site to your right, the path continues with only a rusting fence separating you from the river. After going round the edge of a vast lorry park – the path here has half-width barriers to discourage cyclists – you'll find yourself passing under a network of girders stretching out into the Thames from the forbidding chemical works just inland. The landscape on your right opens up briefly at a signpost, giving a view of scrappy bits of marsh, with horses grazing incongruously on them, and tower blocks in the distance. The path ascends abruptly beside a grim red-brick factory building, then down again past a jumble of towers and industrial sheds, a vast concrete pier system on your left.

Ahead now is the town of Erith, a welcome oasis of human life after the long miles of industrial wasteland.

Turn left up the hill and then left again just before the Playhouse, and down a flight of steps back to the river. The path turns right to follow the river past a housing development and the Erith Deep Water Jetty, now used more by locals taking a stroll than for industrial purposes. Walk round the Erith Deep Water Wharf and continue briefly along the river before the path turns inland along a green fence, then joins a quiet road, James Watt Way.

Turn left down Wheatley Terrace Road, then immediately right up the ramp alongside the cycleway. This road, Appold Street, soon meets a T-junction; turn left into the bigger Manor Road and through a housing development. Continue along

Pier

Pier

Erith Reach

Pier

Pier

Pier

Workings

Rainham Marshe

Mean High Water

Coldharbour Point

house

Mean High Water

Platform

GALLEON C

CHANDLERS DR

WEST STREET

Wharves

Wks

Ocean Park

ERITH

ST FIDELIS ROAD

ROAD

MAXIM ROAD

MANFRED RD

COLCHESTER WAY

MAXIM ROAD

PICKET CLOSE

STONEWOOD RD

WALNUT TREE ROAD

STH

Europa Trading Estate

Erith Sta Station

Car Pk

Liby & Mus

Running Horses

Erith Riverside Gardens

SALMON CL

ERITH HIGH STREET

Pier

Chalk Farm Wharf

Erith Deep Water Jetty

The Playhouse

PO

Garden Wharf

CROSS ST

BEXLEY RD

COLDBLOCK RD

Superstore

THAMES PATH EXTENSION

149

Woolwich to Crayford Ness

Anchor B

CHRISTCHURCH AVENUE

PARK CRES RD

VICTORIA ROAD

PW

Vic

QUEEN ROAD

Car Park

PW

ELRICK C

QUEEN STREET

COMPTON PLACE

PIER RD

PERTH RD

CRESCENT ROAD

JAMES WATT WAY

WHEATLEY RD

APPOLD

Works

MANOR ROAD

LESNEY PARK ROAD

GLEBE W

VICTORIA ROAD

BRITANNIA CLOSE

ALEXANDRA ROAD

SPRINGHEAD ROAD

APERFIELD ROAD

CORNWALLIS C

Pav

Sports

REDDY ROAD

RALEIGH CL

Ed Cen

Anchor Bay
Broken Campshed
The Saltings
Works
Erith Yacht Club
Works
MANOR ROAD
Ppg Sta
Manford Ind Est
Ed Cen
BILTON ROAD
Works
DABBLING CL
CANADA
DUBLIN WAY
LONGREACH ROAD
JENNIFER ROAD
SANDPIPER DRIVE
BEACON ROAD
WALLHOUSE ROAD
Slade Green Schools
ALDERNEY ROAD
GRANGE
SHEPPEY CL
WALLHOUSE ROAD
WIDGEON
Lower Farm
Depot
HILDEN DRIVE
W
War Meml
PLANTATION RD
SLADE GREEN ROAD
PW
RIDGE ROAD
HOLLYWOOD WAY
ROBERT ROAD
MHW
Ind Est
ELM ROAD
HAZEL DRIVE
HAZEL ROAD
HAZEL DRIVE
Pav
Recreation Ground
FOREST ROAD
LEYCROFT
Howbury Farm
Howbury Moat
CLARK
CEDAR ROAD
WILLOW RD
The Glen
Pav
Howbury Farm Cottages
th
d
Slade Green Station
PO
Crayford Mars
on Gd
Station
MOAT LANE
OAK
Slade Green

Manor Road for half a mile or so, past warehouses, a recycling depot and an unexpected blue weatherboarded complex housing Erith Safety. A large waste-management site follows, and Erith Trading Estate leads off on your right.

This is not the most scenic section of the path, but don't despair – a hundred yards or so after Aggregate Industries a sign points left to Erith Yacht Club. Follow it down a small, pleasingly overgrown lane, and right at the bottom down an even

Elizabeth II Bridge, which carries the M25 southbound over the Thames, hence representing the boundary between London and the outside world. This spot is Crayford Ness, the official end of the Thames Path.

You can allow yourself a moment of self-congratulation, but there's still more than a mile to the nearest station. After a couple of hundred yards the path curves in again. Follow it round alongside what is now Dartford Creek, which forms the mouth of the River Darent. On your left is Dartford Creek Tidal Barrier, a cousin to the similar but larger structure at Barking. Turning your back to the Thames, pass through a steel gate and keep along the path. When level with the barrier you pass through another gate, across an approach road and back on to the continuation of the same path. As Dartford Creek bends right the path follows it through another gate and on – towards the end of the day you'll be walking straight into the setting sun. The path keeps on for ½ mile (0.8 km) or so, leaving behind the industrial estate and continuing through timeless marshland with its long grasses and piping birds.

At a junction, keep straight on, leaving the Creek behind, and descend gently to a narrow lane with thick hedges on either side. Continue on this lane for another ½ mile (0.8 km); you'll then encounter a moated house, quite ruined: this is Howbury Moat, which dates back all the way to the 11th century, when it was occupied by Odo, Bishop of Bayeux and half-brother of William the Conqueror.

Pass through a gate and keep straight on; you'll soon emerge on to Moat Lane. Turn left down the lane and continue in the same direction for 100 yards (90 metres), until you see a footbridge and a car park to your right. This is Slade Green station, and the end of your travels.

narrower lane, with peaceful marshland to your right, until you pass through a gateway and find yourself on a raised earth bank that doubles as a sea wall. To your left is the yacht club, to your right marshes with grazing cattle and Second World War pillboxes – this is Erith Saltings, the last remaining fragment of salt marsh on the London Thames.

Follow the track for a couple of hundred yards and you'll find yourself by the Thames again, though at the price of an unattractive scrapyard on your right. Beyond it is a pylon with a constantly revolving bar – this is a radar station that observes shipping and feeds back the details to the vessel control room by the Thames Barrier. As you pass it, the track curves right between low concrete walls, and not far ahead you can see the Queen

Useful Information

Transport

The Thames Path in London is easily accessible by public transport. The Transport for London website (www.tfl.gov.uk; tel. 020 7222 1234) has detailed maps and service information for all tube, Docklands Light Railway, London Overground, bus and Thames Clipper routes. Mainline rail services to and from the western section of the London Thames are run by South West Trains (www.southwesttrains.co.uk), and to the eastern section by Southern Railway (www.southernrailway.com). There are timetable details for all mainline rail services at www.nationalrail.co.uk (tel. 08457 484950). Engineering works are common at weekends on train, tube and DLR lines alike, so check the relevant websites before you set off.

Rather than buying individual tickets for each leg of the journey, it is usually easiest and cheapest to use an Oyster card; these can be bought at tube and DLR stations and topped up as necessary at any station or in newsagents displaying the Oyster sign. Oyster cards are valid on all train, tube, DLR, London Overground and bus services within Greater London, and also on Thames Clippers, but not on any other boat services.

Boat services

There are many passenger boat services that run along the Thames.

Thames Clippers Embankment to Woolwich Arsenal, calling at Blackfriars, Bankside, London Bridge, Tower, Canary Wharf, Greenland, Masthouse Terrace, Greenwich and North Greenwich. Also 'Tate to Tate' service from Vauxhall/Millbank to Bankside/Blackfriars, and Canary Wharf to Hilton Docklands Rotherhithe.
ⓘ www.thamesclippers.com/
☎ 0870 781 5049

Thames River Boats Hampton Court to Westminster, calling at Richmond and Kew. April to October only.
ⓘ www.wpsa.co.uk
☎ 020 7930 2062

Thames River Services Westminster to the Thames Barrier, calling at St Katharine's and Greenwich.
ⓘ www.thamesriverservices.co.uk
☎ 020 7930 4097

Hammerton's Ferry Twickenham to Ham.
ⓘ www.hammertonsferry.co.uk
☎ 020 8892 9620

Turks Launches Hampton Court to Richmond via Kingston. April to October only.
ⓘ www.turks.co.uk
☎ 020 8546 2434

Useful contacts

Thames Path official website
ⓘ www.nationaltrail.co.uk/thamespath
☎ 01865 810224

Useful unofficial website
ⓘ www.thames-path-org.uk

Walk London As well as the Thames Path, the Walk London website also includes information about the Capital Ring, London Loop, Lea Valley Walk, Green Chain Walk, Jubilee Walkway and Jubilee Greenway.
ⓘ www.walklondon.org.uk/route.asp?R=6

Visit London Official tourist board, with details of accommodation and sites to see: 1 Lower Regent Street, London SW1 4XT
ⓘ www.visitlondon.com
☎ 08701 566 366

Kingston Tourist Information Centre The Market House, Market Place, Kingston-upon-Thames KT1 1JS
ⓘ www.kingston.gov.uk/browse/leisure/tourism.htm
☎ 020 8546 1140

Twickenham Visitor Information Centre
44 York Street, Twickenham TW1 3BZ
ⓘ www.visitrichmond.co.uk
☎ 020 8891 7272

Greenwich Tourist Information Centre
Pepys House, 2 Cutty Sark Gardens,
Greenwich SE10 9LW
ⓘ www.visitgreenwich.org.uk
☎ 0870 6082000

Tide Times Tide tables for the UK.
ⓘ www.tidetimes.org.uk

River Thames Society Registered charity
devoted to supporting and protecting the
Thames from source to sea.
ⓘ www.riverthamessociety.org.uk
☎ 01491 612456

Further reading

A select list; all out-of-print books can be bought via www.abebooks.co.uk. Dates refer to
original publication.

Non-fiction

Peter Ackroyd, *London: The Biography* (Chatto & Windus, 2000)

Peter Ackroyd, *Thames: Sacred River* (Chatto & Windus, 2007)

Brian Cookson, *Crossing the River: The History of London's Thames River Bridges from
Richmond to the Tower* (Mainstream, 2006)

Graham Diprose, Charles Craig and Mike Seaborne, *London's Changing Riverscape:
Panoramas from London Bridge to Greenwich* (Frances Lincoln, 2009)

A. P. Herbert, *The Thames* (Weidenfeld & Nicolson, 1966, o/p)

John Marriot, *Beyond the Tower: A History of East London* (Yale University Press, 2011)

Nikolaus Pevsner and successors, *The Buildings of England: London* (six volumes; Yale
University Press, 1983–2005)

Roy Porter, *London: A Social History* (Penguin, 1995)

Jonathan Schneer, *The Thames: England's River* (Little, Brown, 2005)

Gillian Tindall, *The House by the Thames: and the People Who Lived There* (Chatto & Windus,
2006)

Jerry White, *London in the Eighteenth Century* (Bodley Head, 2012)

Jerry White, *London in the Nineteenth Century* (Jonathan Cape, 2007)

Jerry White, *London in the Twentieth Century* (Vintage, 2008)

Fiction

Ben Aaronovitch, *Rivers of London* (Gollancz, 2011)

William Boyd, *Ordinary Thunderstorms* (Bloomsbury, 2009)

Arthur Conan Doyle, *The Sign of Four* (Penguin, 1890)

Charles Dickens, *Great Expectations* (Penguin, 1861)

Charles Dickens, *Oliver Twist* (Penguin, 1838)

Charles Dickens, *Our Mutual Friend* (Penguin, 1865).

Jerome K. Jerome, *Three Men in a Boat* (Penguin, 1889)

Matthew Kneale, *Sweet Thames* (Penguin, 1992)

Iris Murdoch, *Bruno's Dream* (Vintage, 1969)

Iain Sinclair, *Downriver* (Penguin, 1991)

Useful Information

Acknowledgements

My thanks first of all to Graham Coster of Aurum Press for the opportunity to write this book, and for steering it so smoothly through the editorial process. I'd like to pay tribute to Robert Updegraff for his meticulous design work, Brenda Updegraff for her helpful editing and Katherine Clarke for taking most of the photographs in this book – a major enterprise with some fantastic results.

I'm also grateful to Jenny Humphreys at Walk London, to David Garrard for his unstinting and enormously valuable architectural help, and to my father Christopher Clapham for casting his eagle eye over the proofs. Many thanks to my colleagues at the London office of Yale University Press for their interest and support; Yale's impressive list of British art and architectural history books has also been an exceptionally useful resource in the writing of this book.

Finally, I'd like to thank all those who gave up their time to test out sections of the book, offering countless helpful suggestions and corrections in the process: Tom Buhler and Charlotte Stafford, Eric Dickson, David and Holly Garrard, Andrew Harvey, Toby Hawks, Lucy Okell and Cathy Robinson, Kate Pocock, Tanya Wright and Tilda Yolland. Any remaining mistakes of course are mine.

Picture Credits

Definitive guides to popular long-distance walks published by

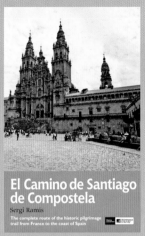

Aurum

El Camino de Santiago de Compostela
Sergi Ramis

The complete route of the historic pilgrimage trail from France to the coast of Spain

ISBN 978 1 84513 708 3

The Capital Ring
Colin Saunders

78 miles of green corridor encircling inner London

ISBN 978 1 84513 786 1

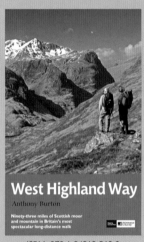

West Highland Way
Anthony Burton

Ninety-three miles of Scottish moor and mountain in Britain's most spectacular long-distance walk

ISBN 978 1 84513 569 0

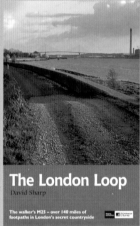

The London Loop
David Sharp

The walker's M25 – over 140 miles of footpaths in London's secret countryside

ISBN 978 1 84513 787 8

The Coast to Coast Walk
Martin Wainwright

The classic high-level walk from Irish Sea to North Sea

ISBN 978 1 84513 560 7

The Official Guides to all o

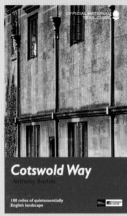

Cotswold Way
Anthony Burton

100 miles of quintessentially
English landscape

ISBN 978 1 84513 785 4

Cleveland Way
Ian Sampson

Over 100 miles of magnificent
walking on the North York Moors

ISBN 978 1 84513 781 6

Pennine Way
Damian Hall

The whole of England's toughest
National Trail

ISBN 978 1 84513 718 2

Yorkshire Wolds Way
Roger Ratcliffe

A superbly tranquil walk through the
unspoilt chalk hills of East Yorkshire

ISBN 978 1 84513 643 7

**Pembrokeshire
Coast Path**
Brian John

180 miles of clifftop, beach and cove
around the magnificent Welsh coast

ISBN 978 1 84513 602 4

South Downs Way
Paul Millmore

100 miles of glorious chalk downland
for the walker, cyclist and horse rider

ISBN 978 1 84513 565 2

Hadrian's Wall Path
Anthony Burton

Follow the Roman Wall
from coast to coast

ISBN 978 1 84513 567 6

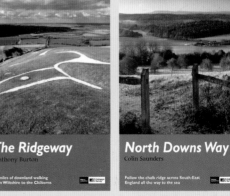

The Ridgeway
Anthony Burton

87 miles of downland walking
from Wiltshire to the Chilterns

ISBN 978 1 84513 638 3

North Downs Way
Colin Saunders

Follow the chalk ridge across South-East
England all the way to the sea

ISBN 978 1 84513 677 2